I0477654

This Coloring Book Belongs To:

____

____

Color Chart

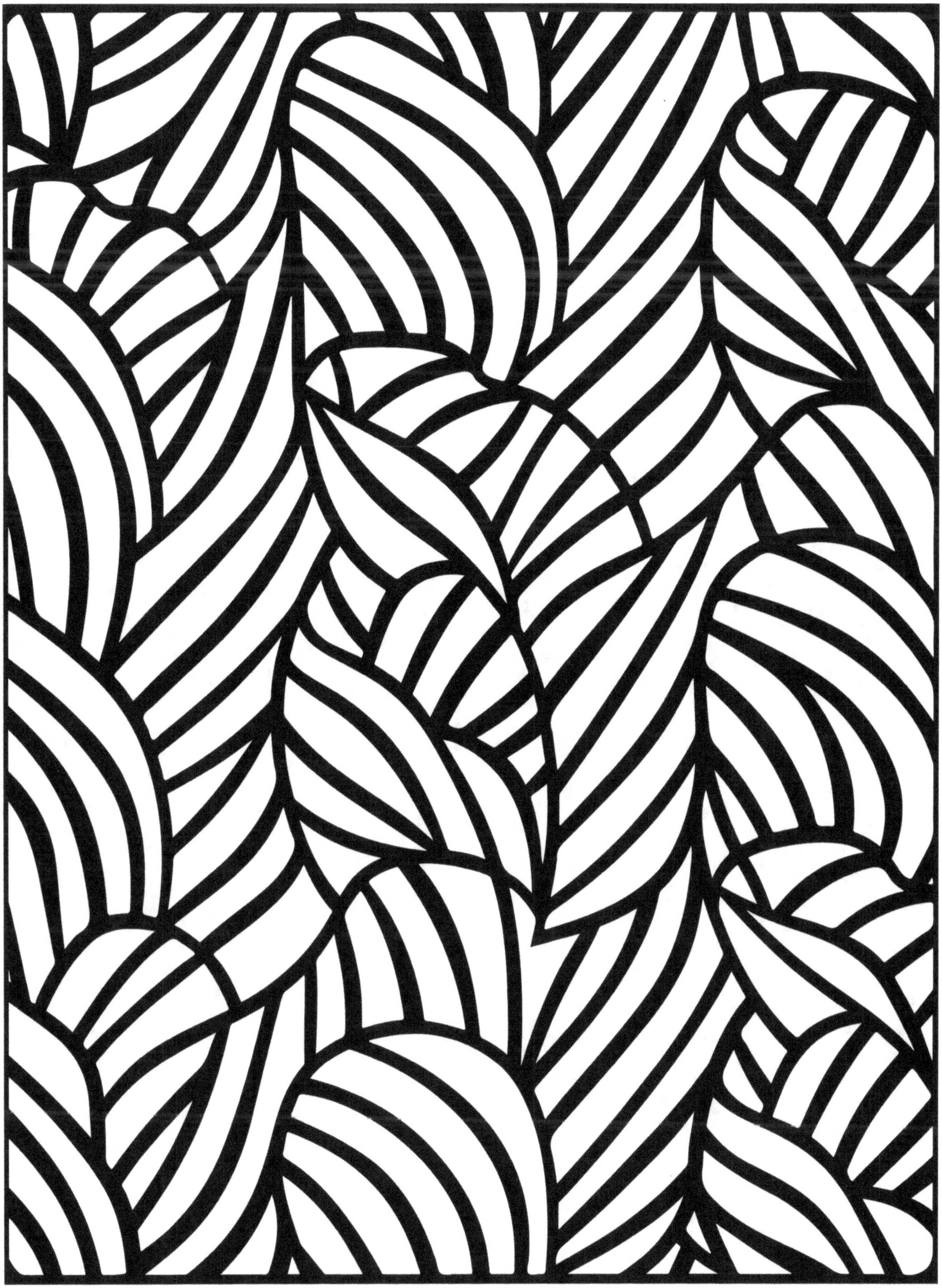

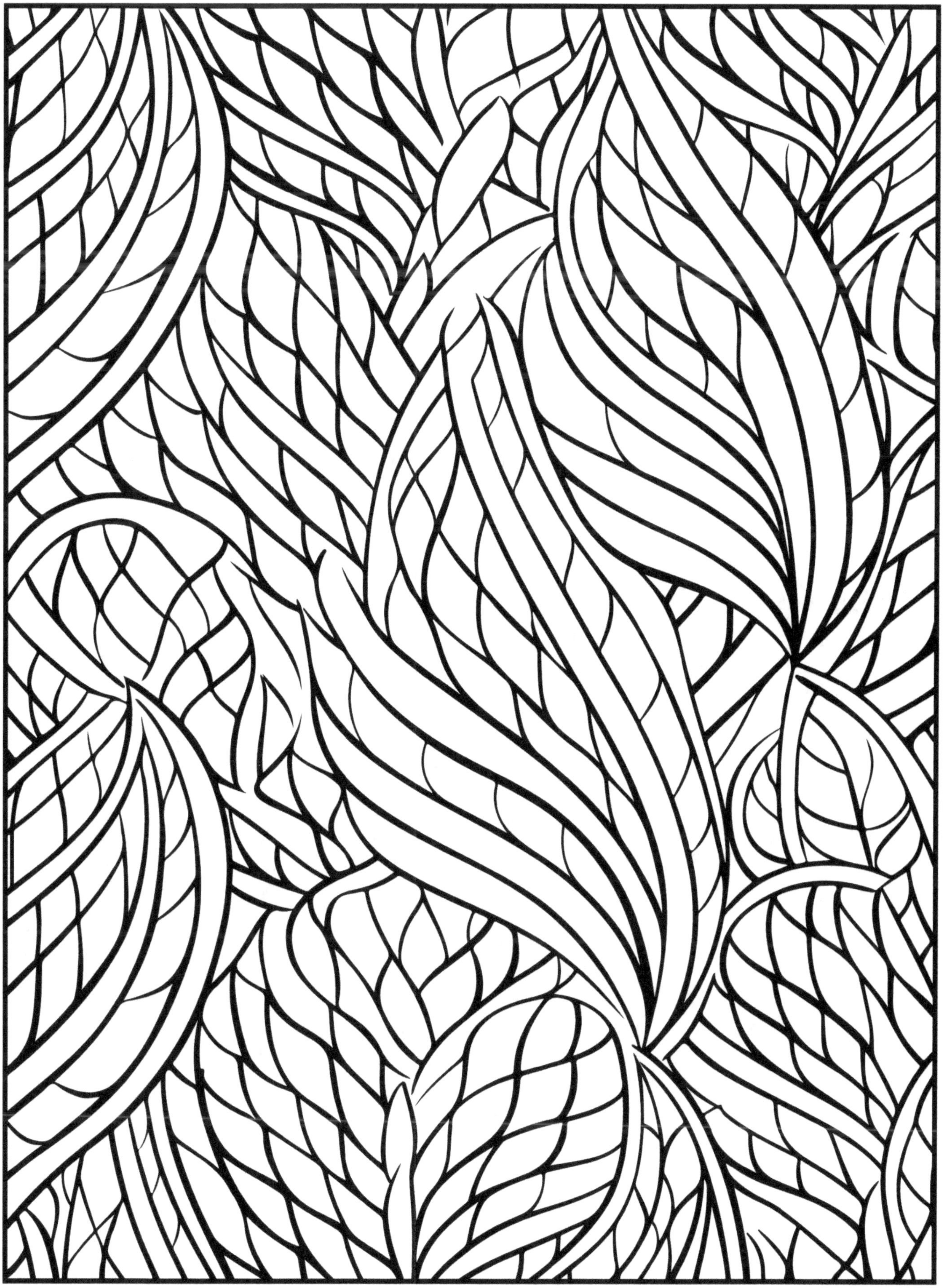

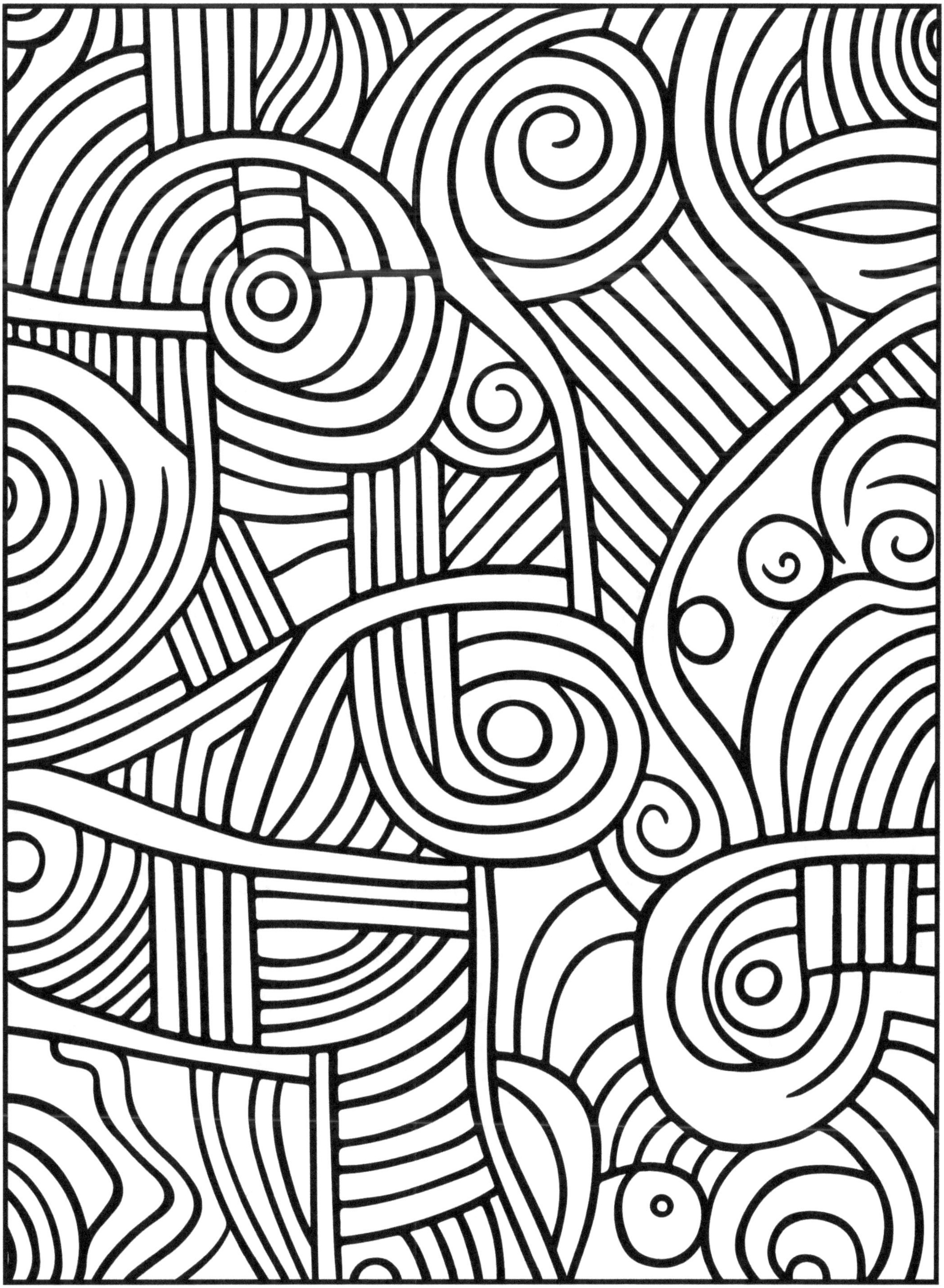

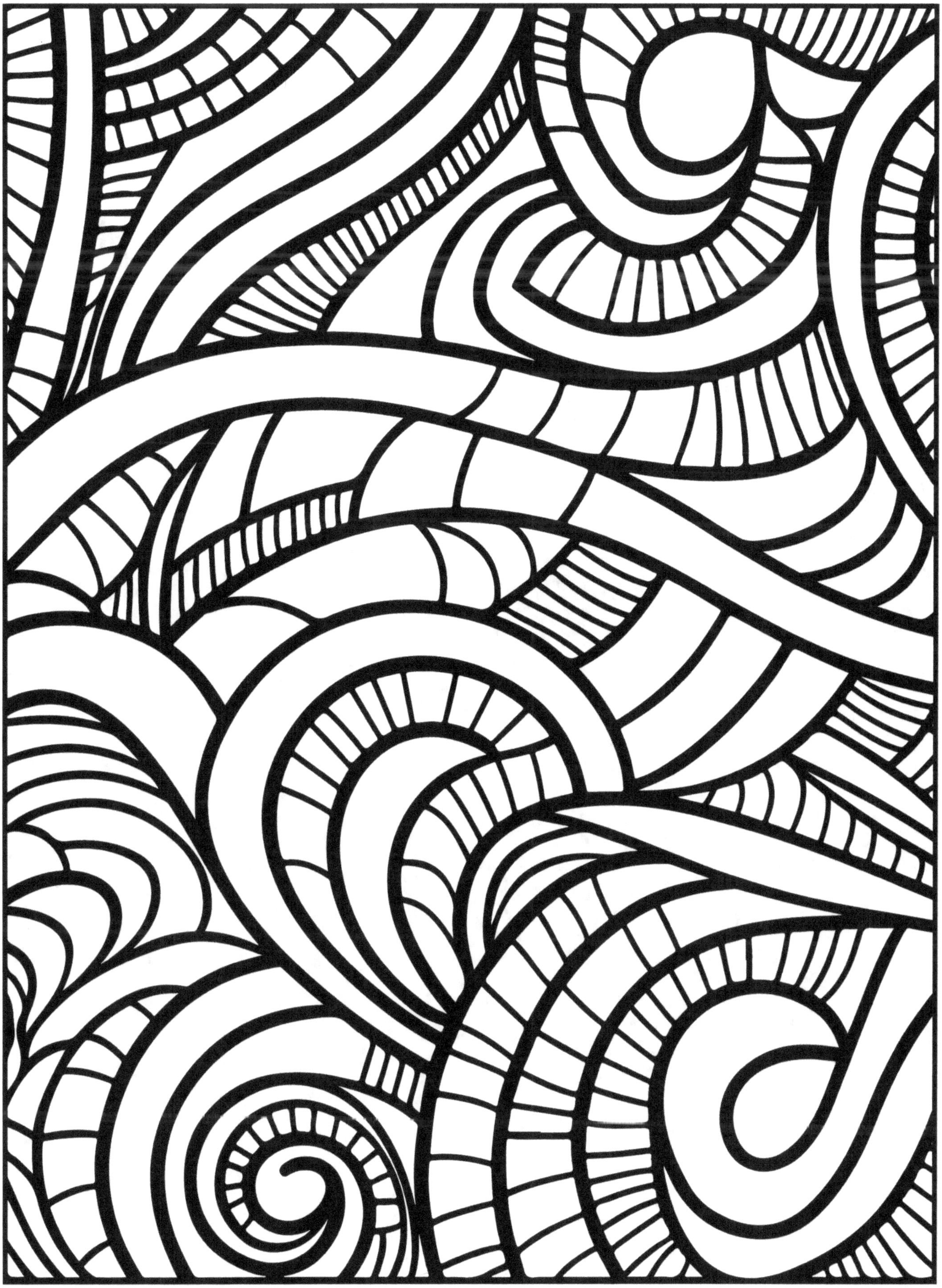

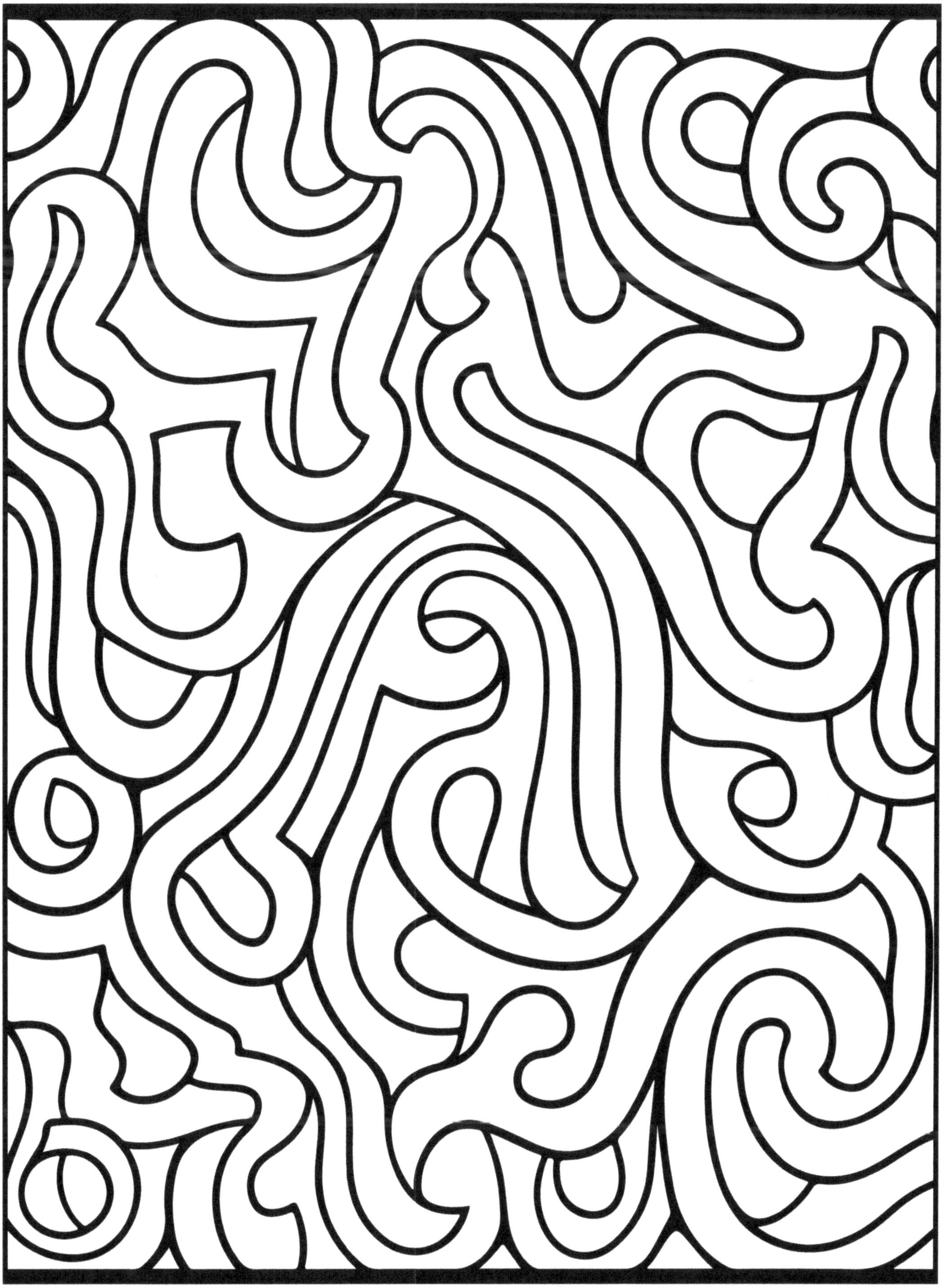

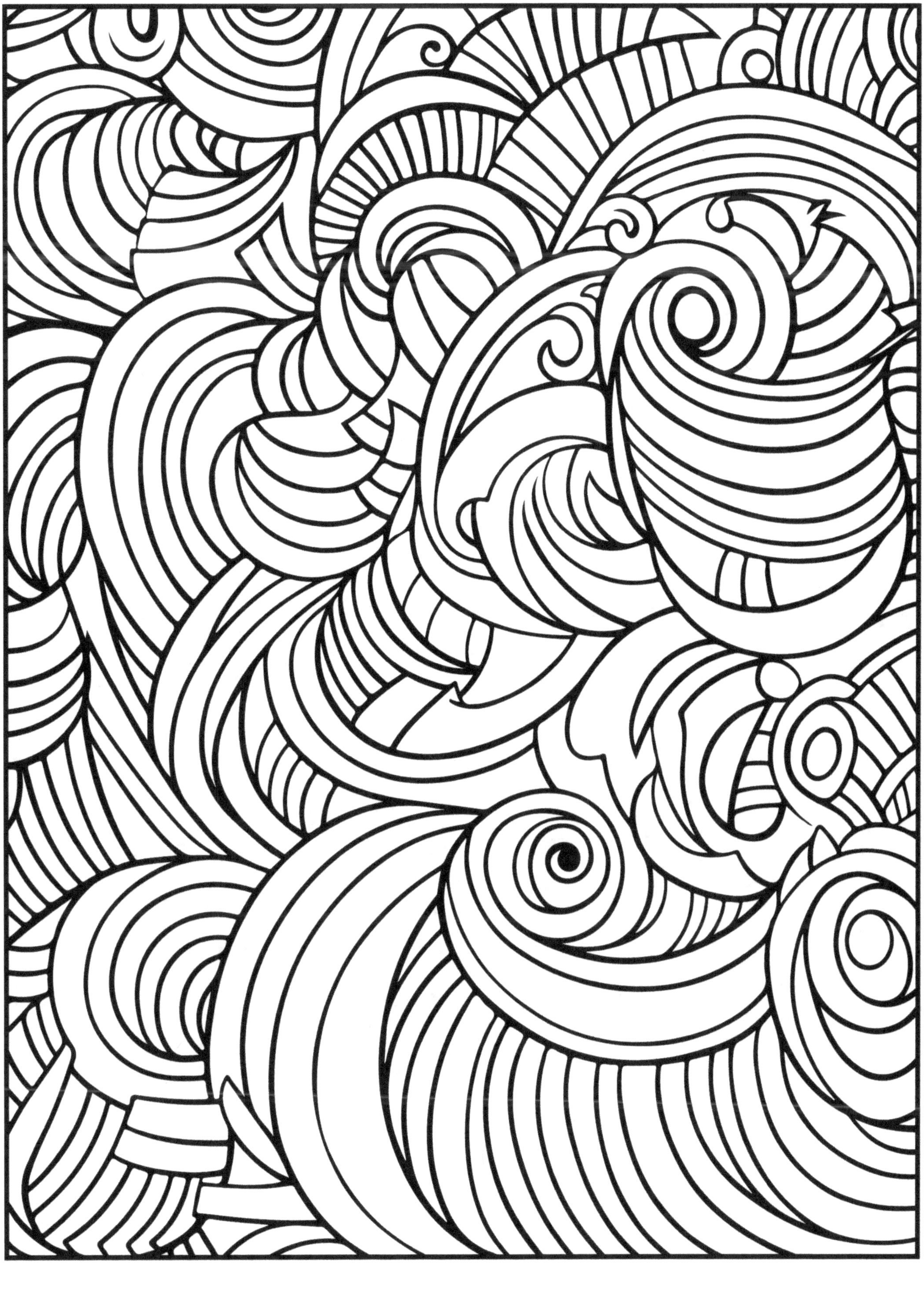

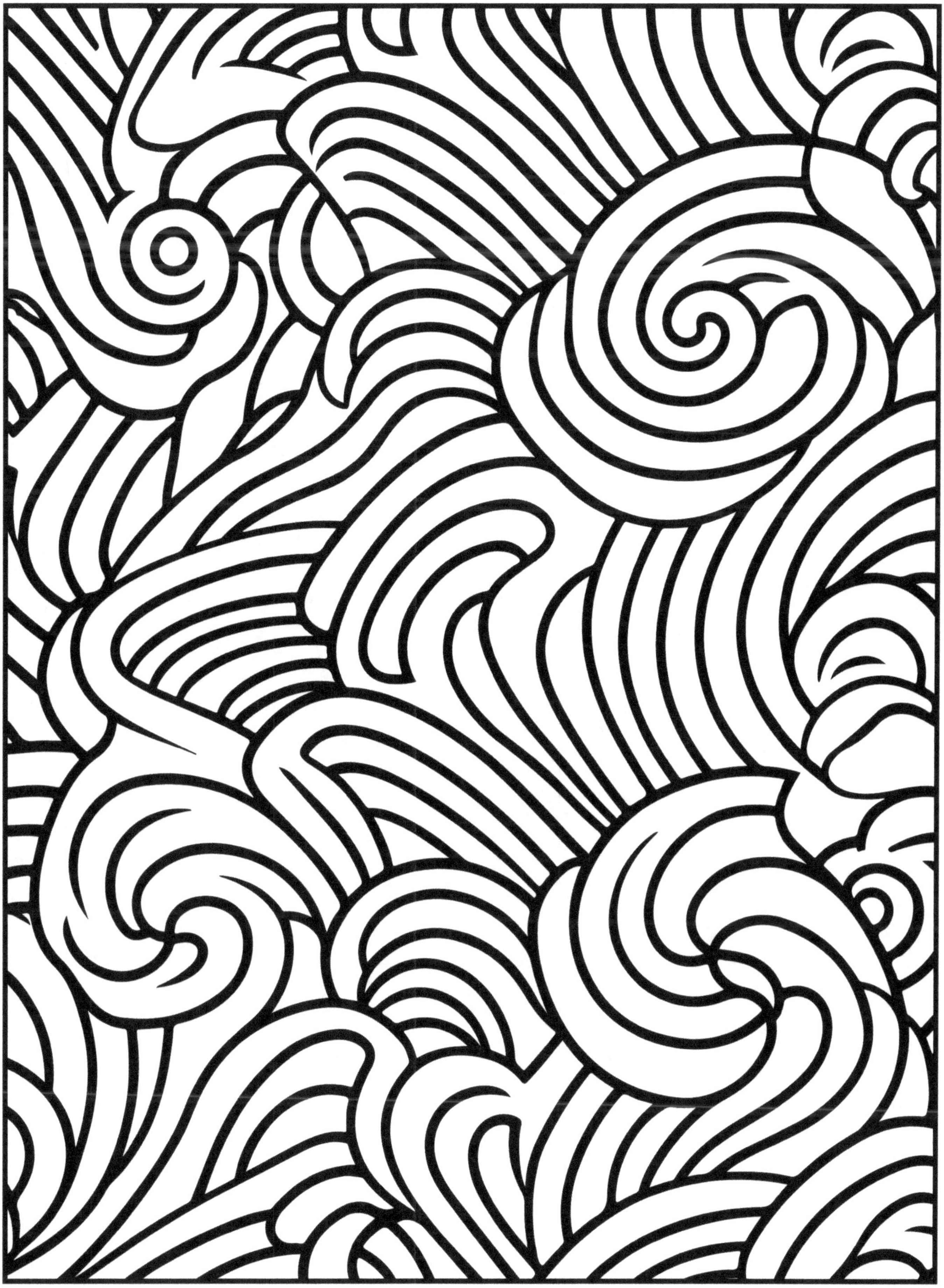

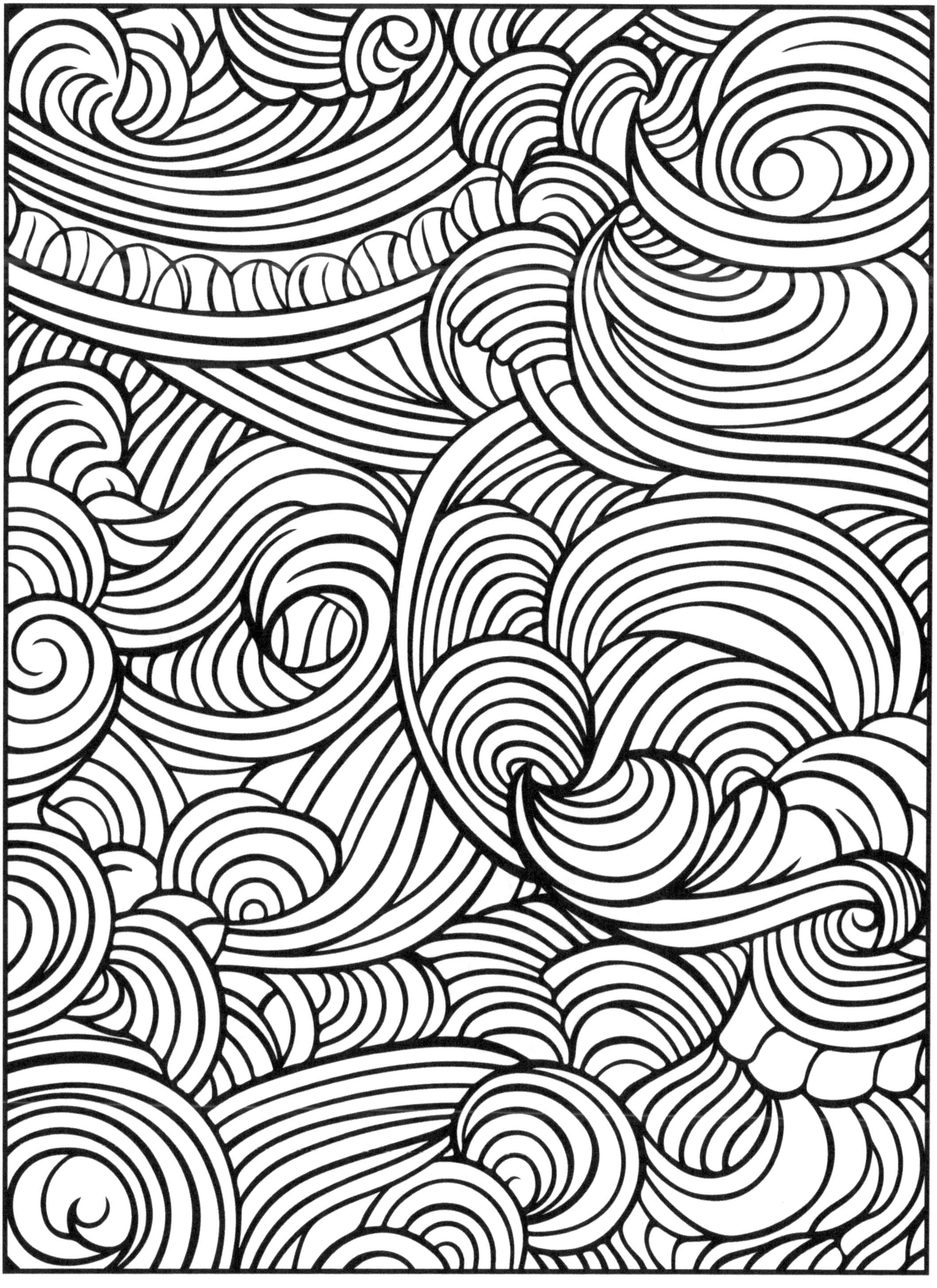

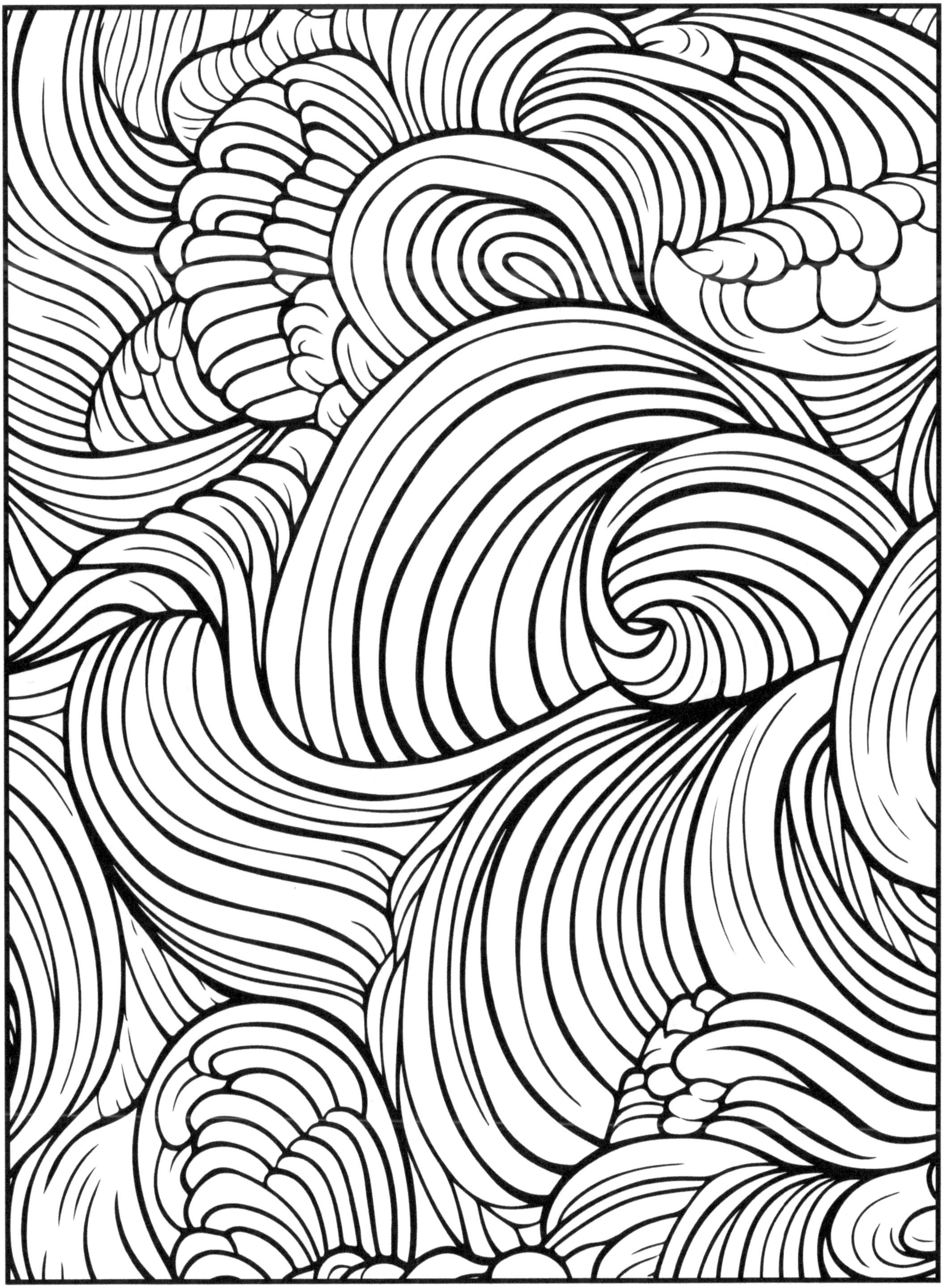

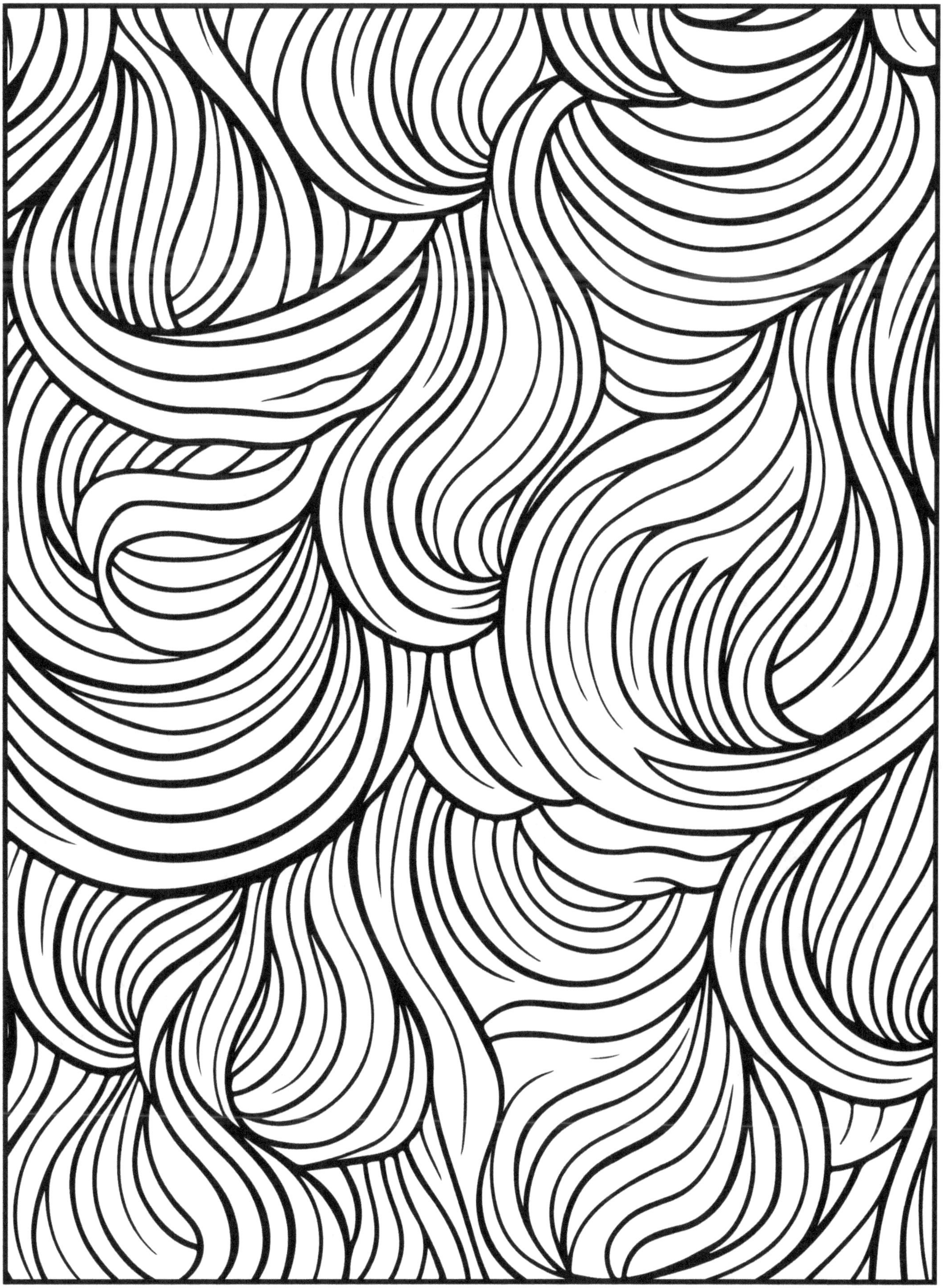

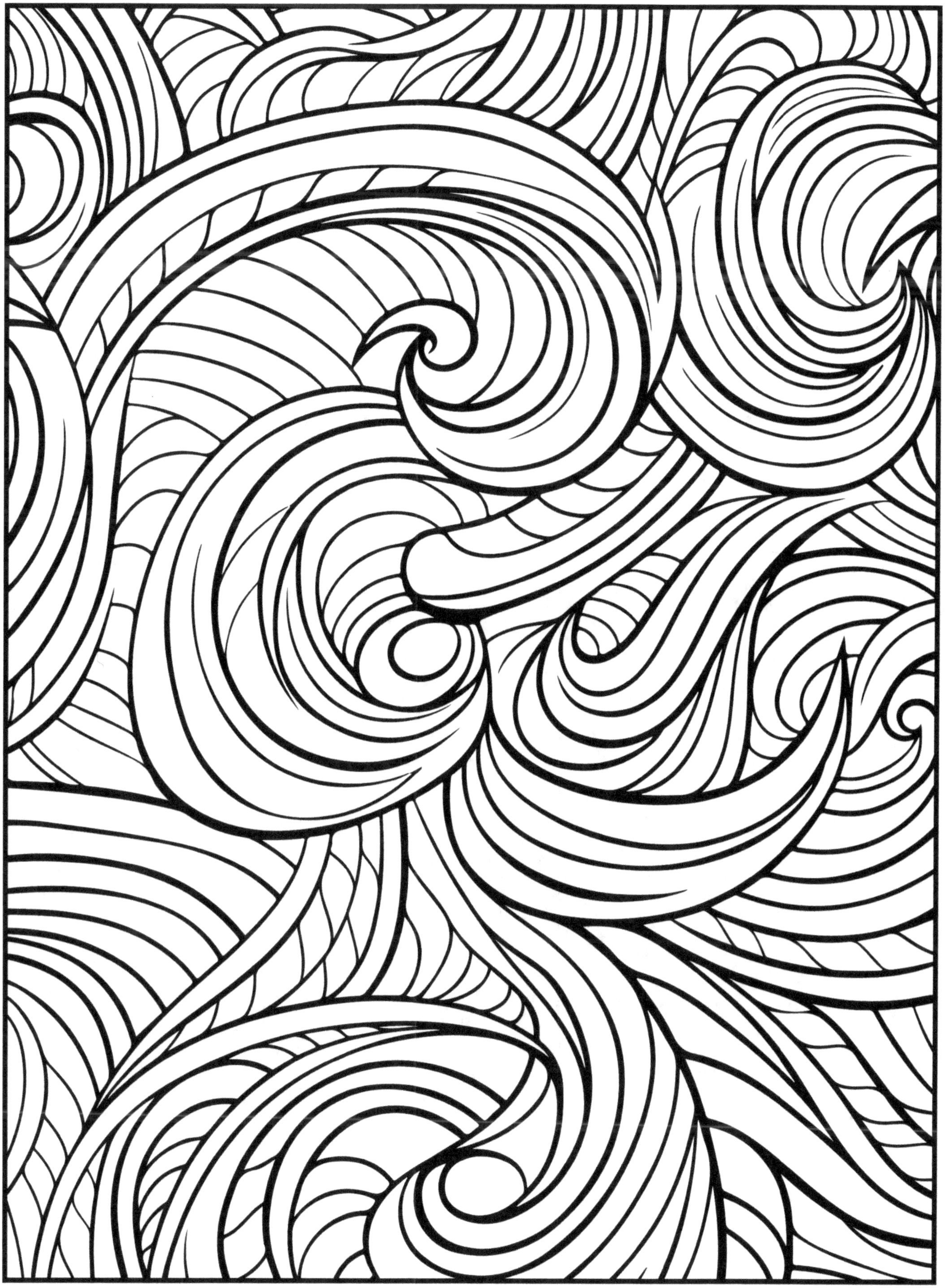

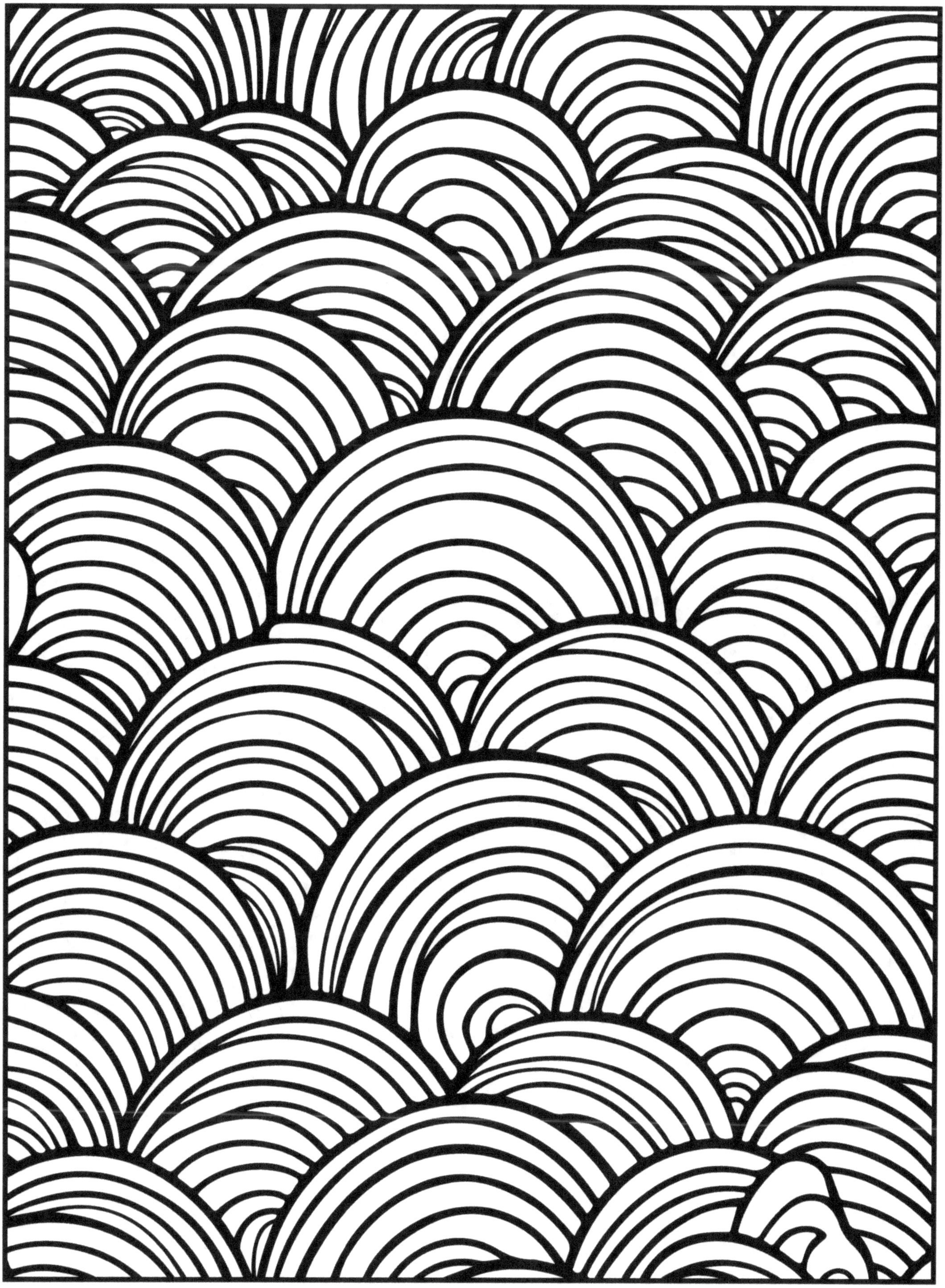

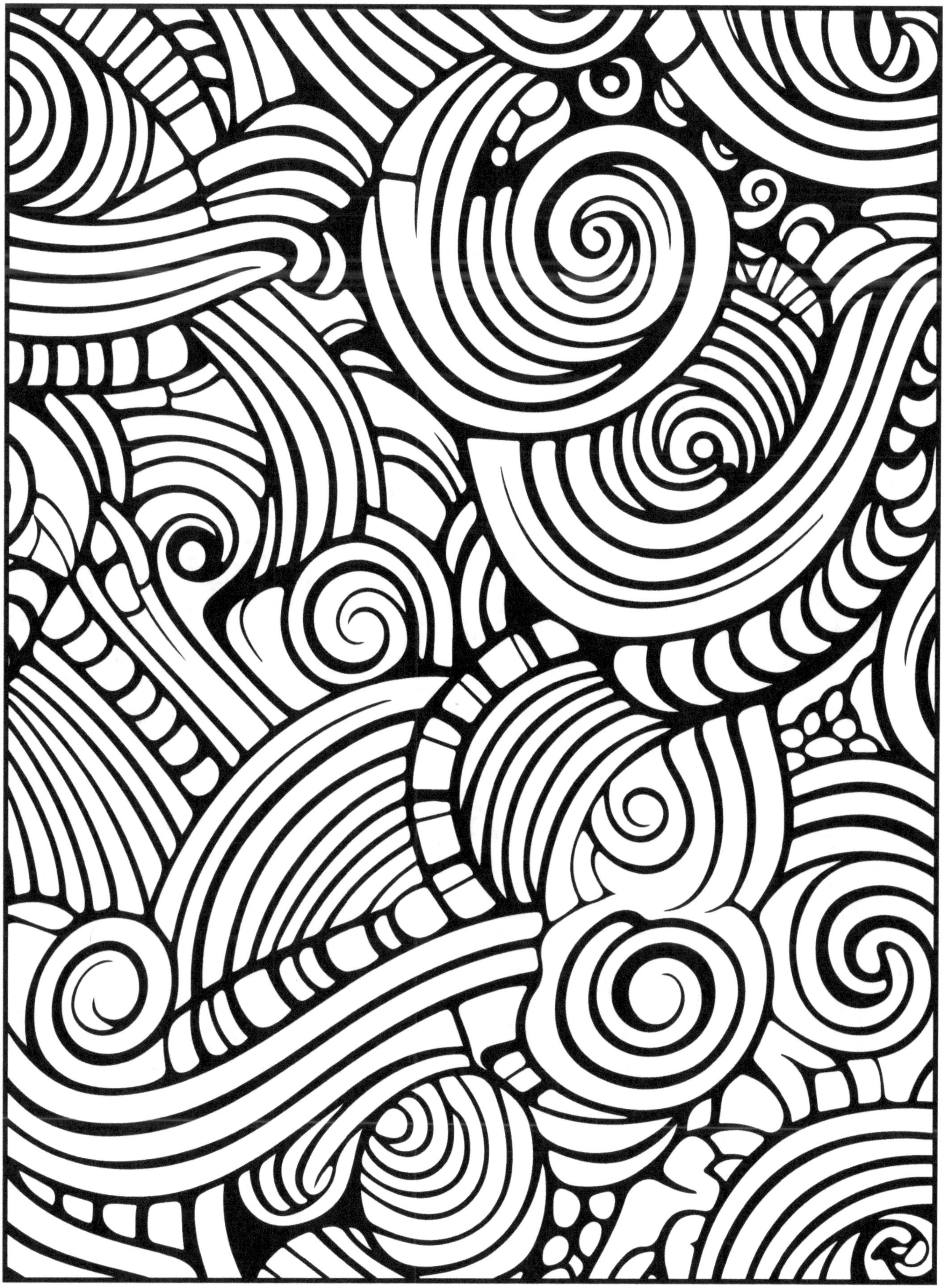

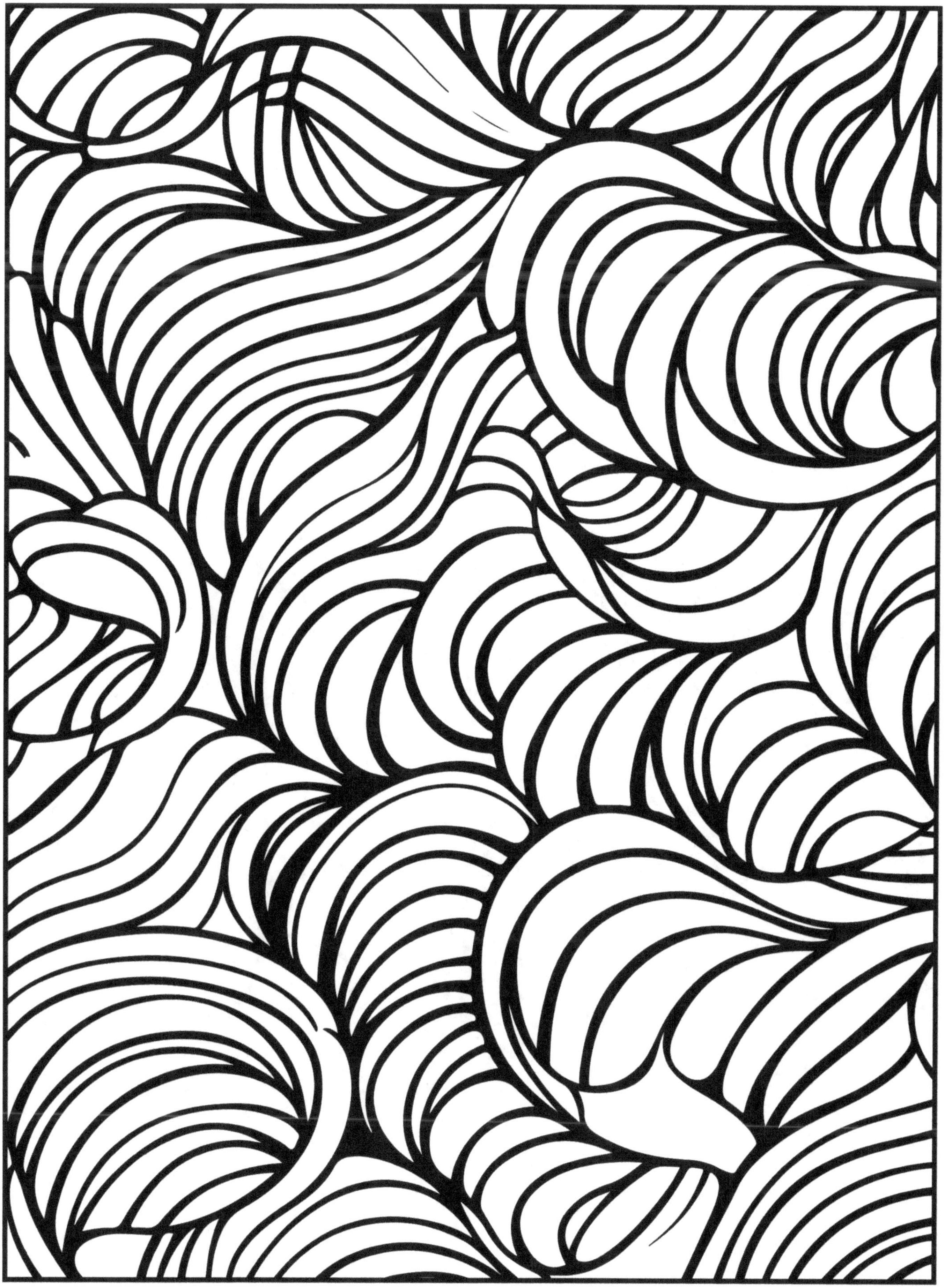

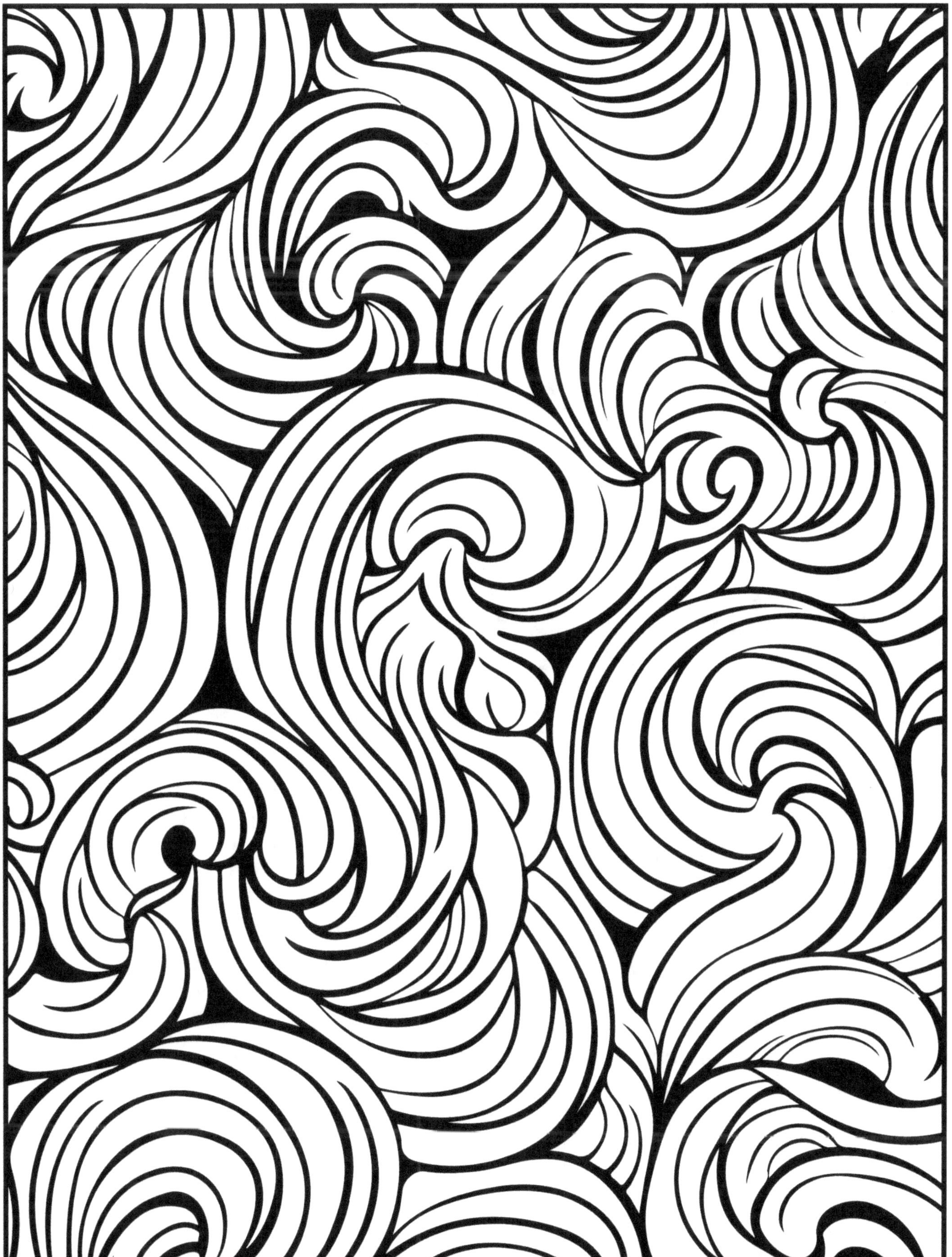

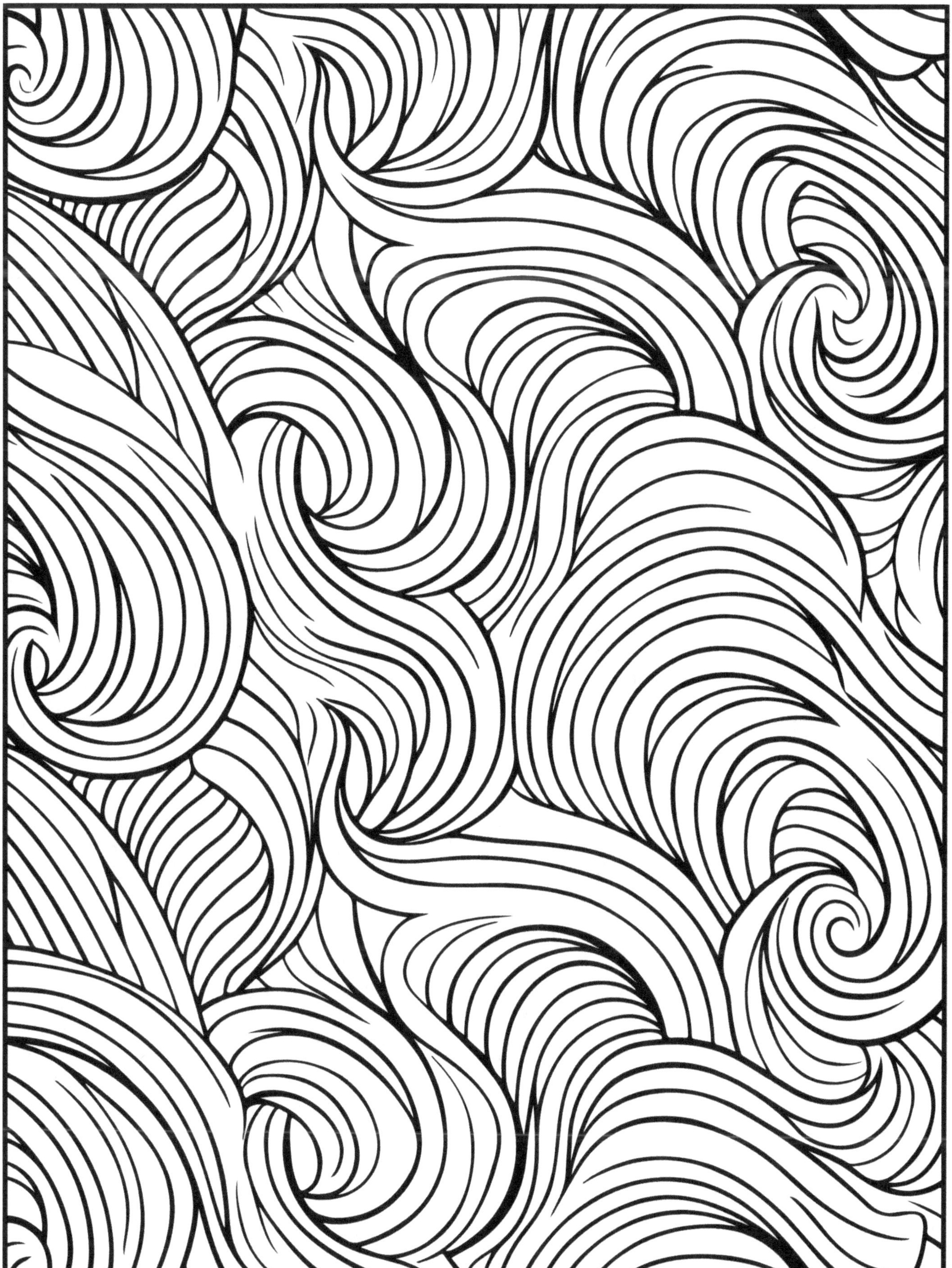

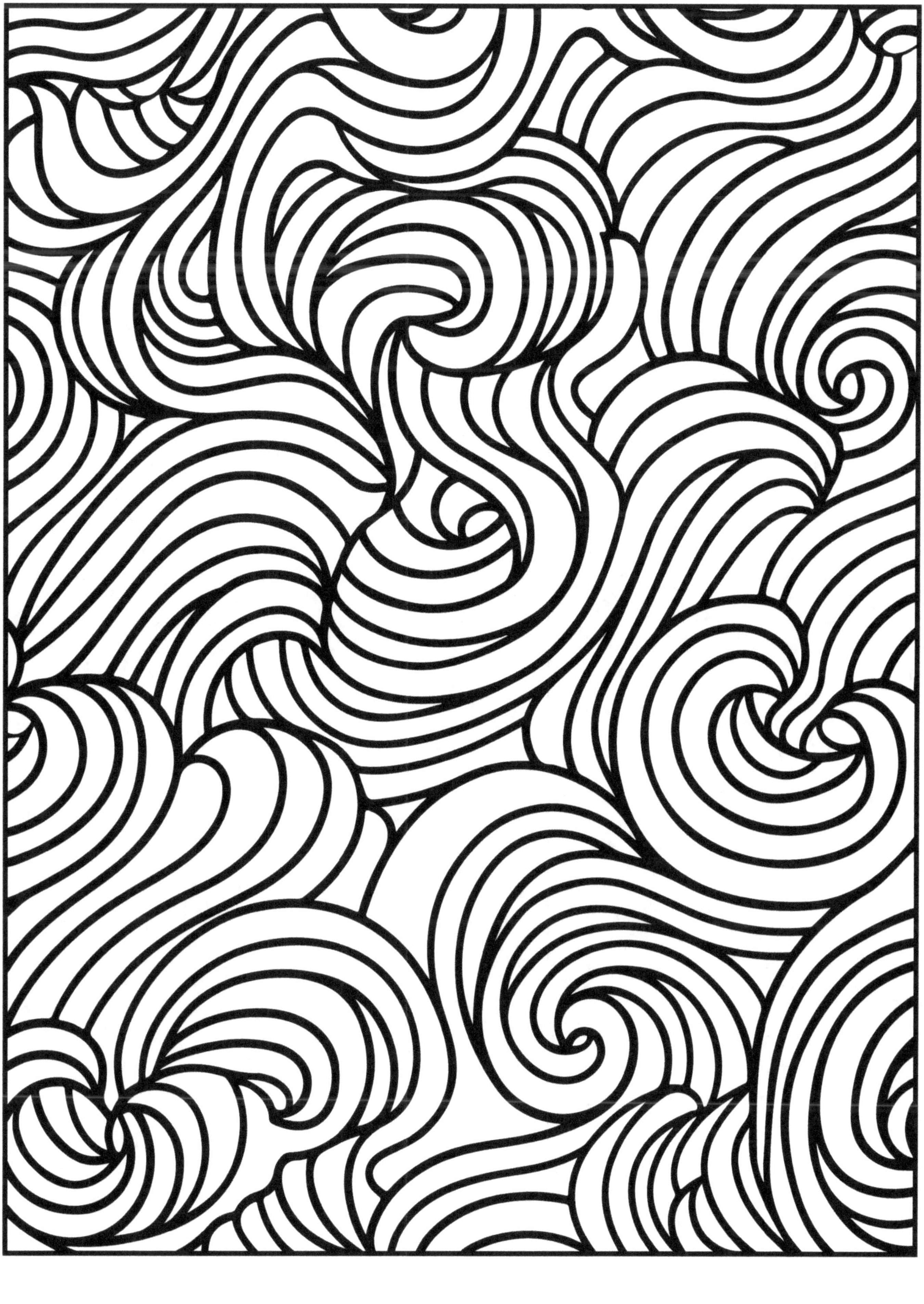

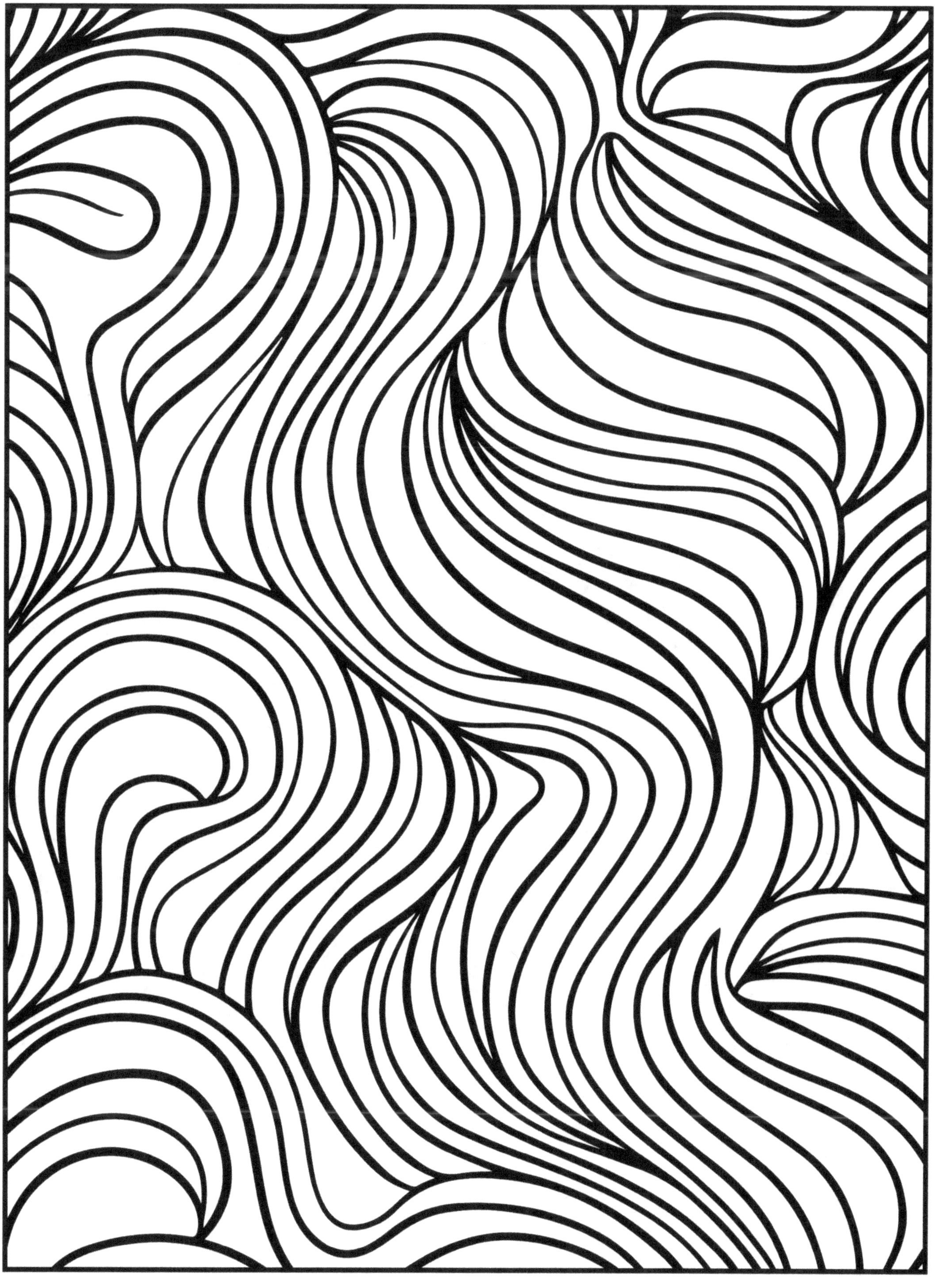

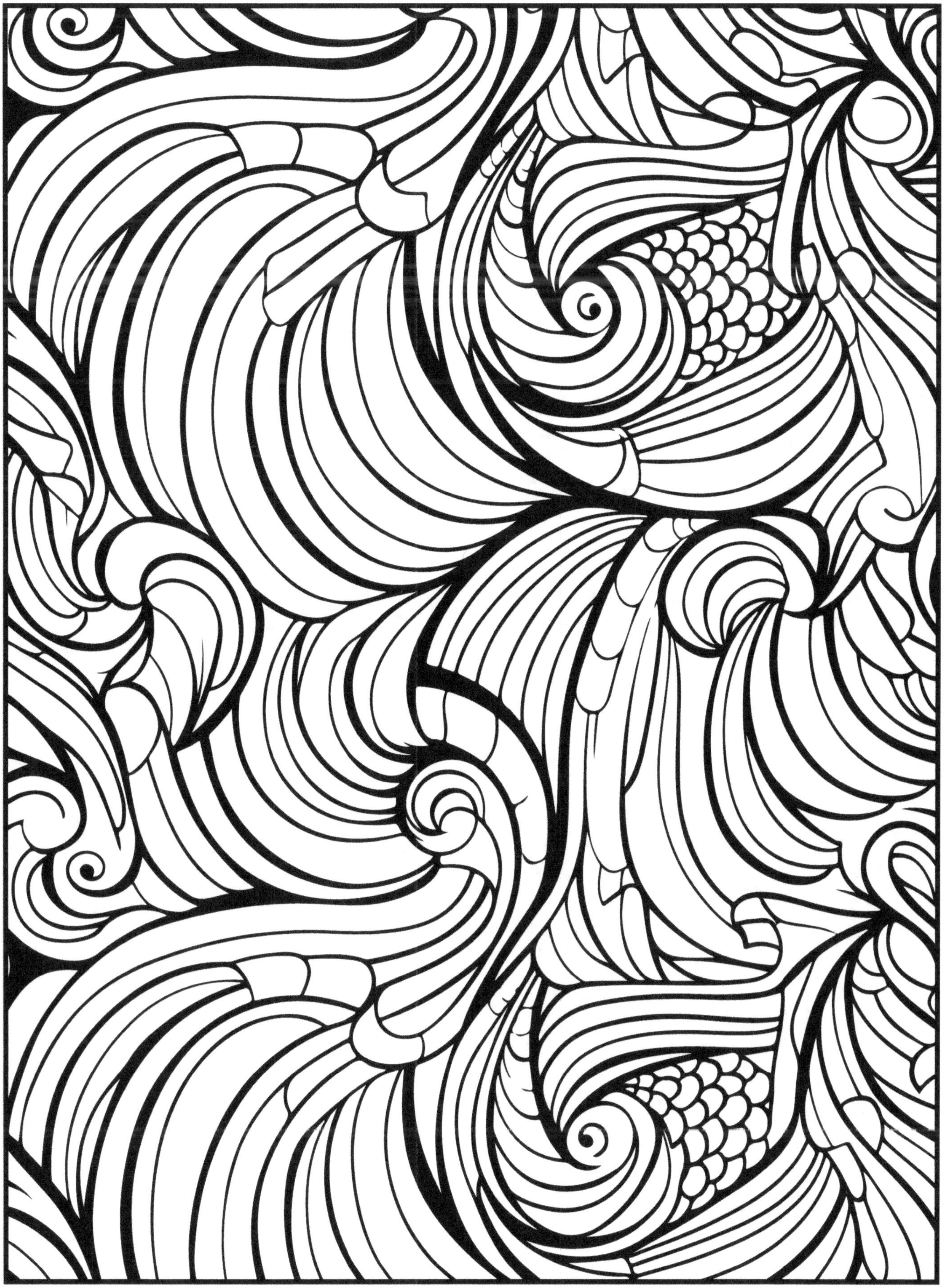

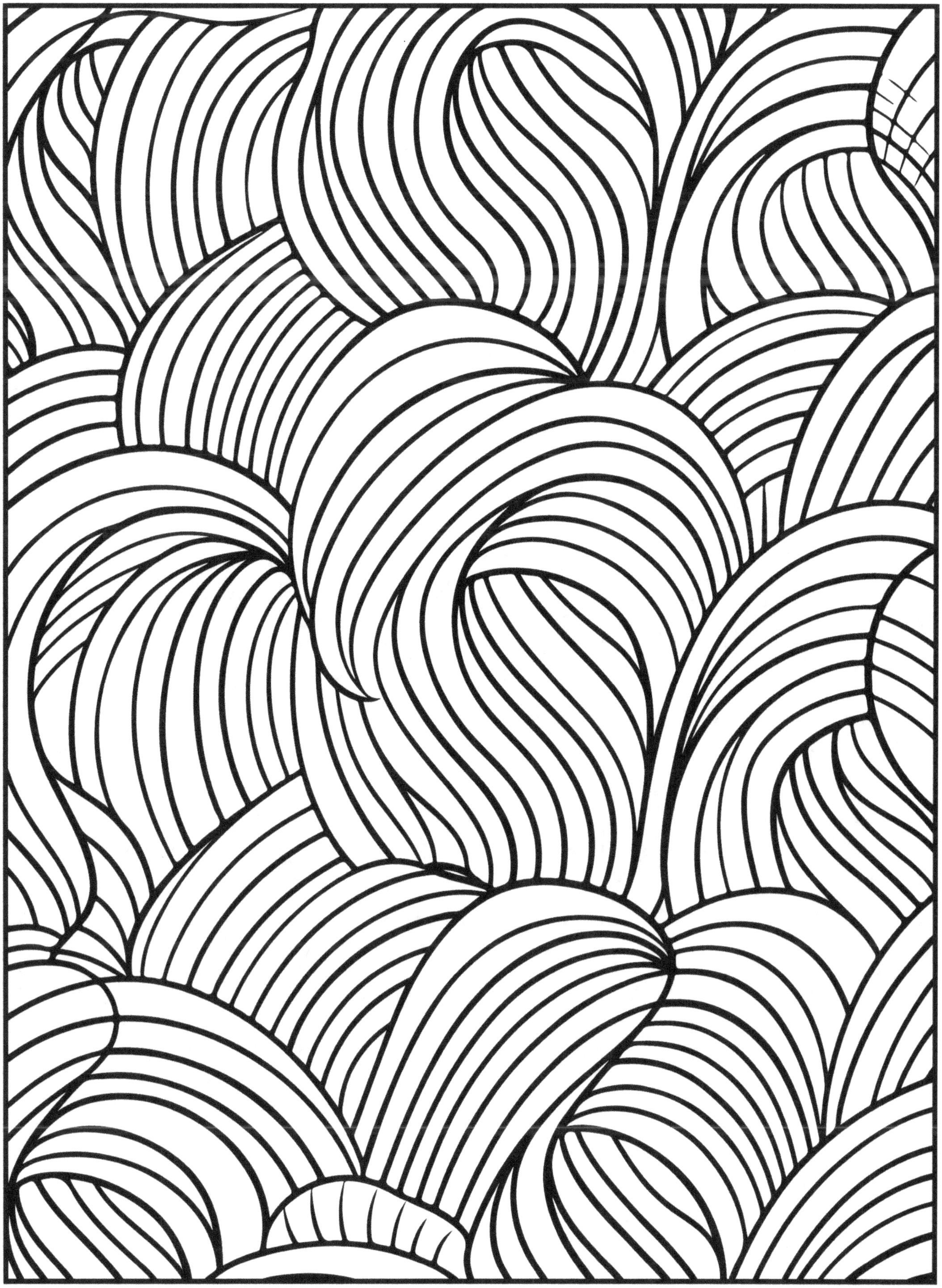

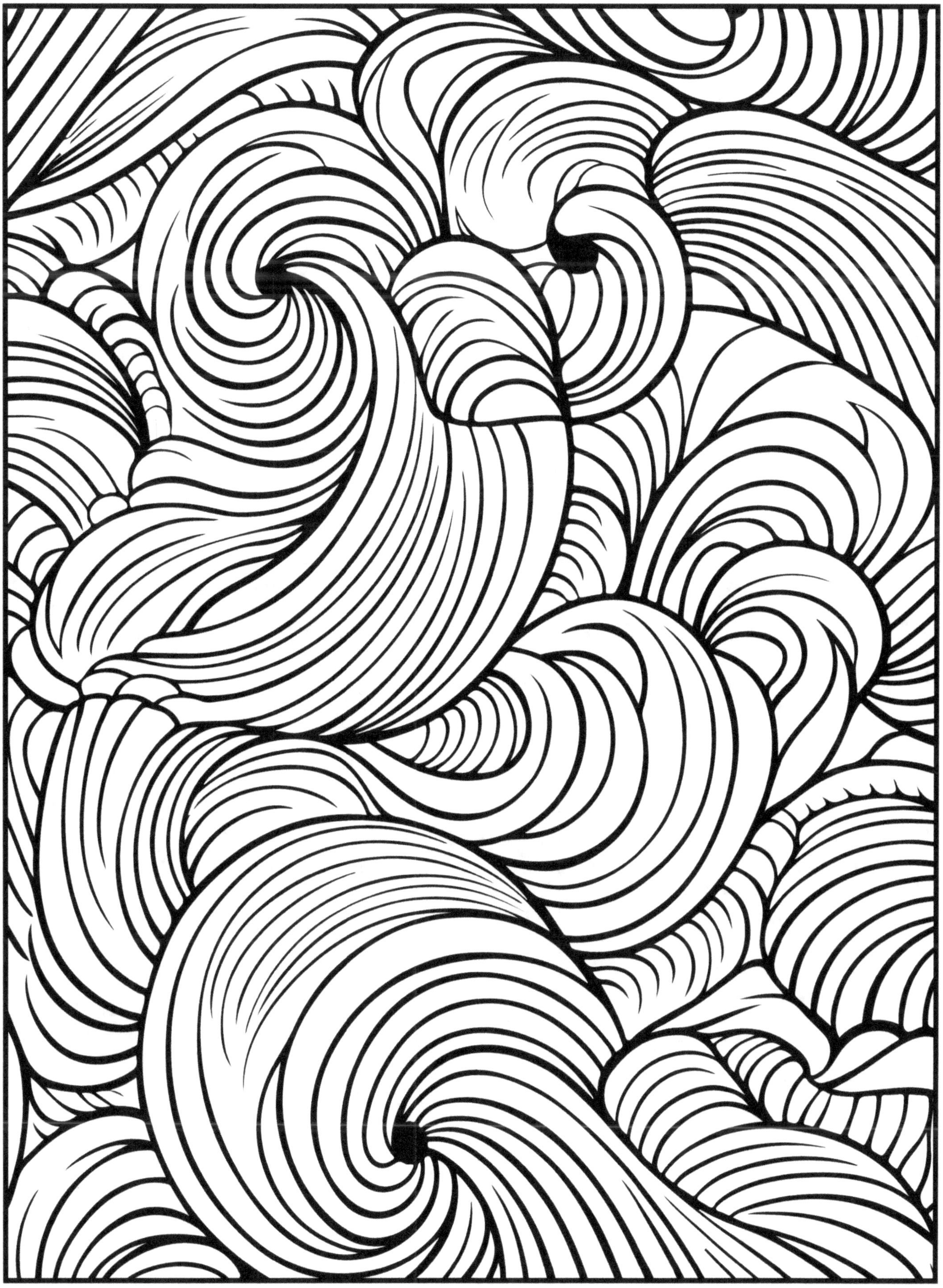

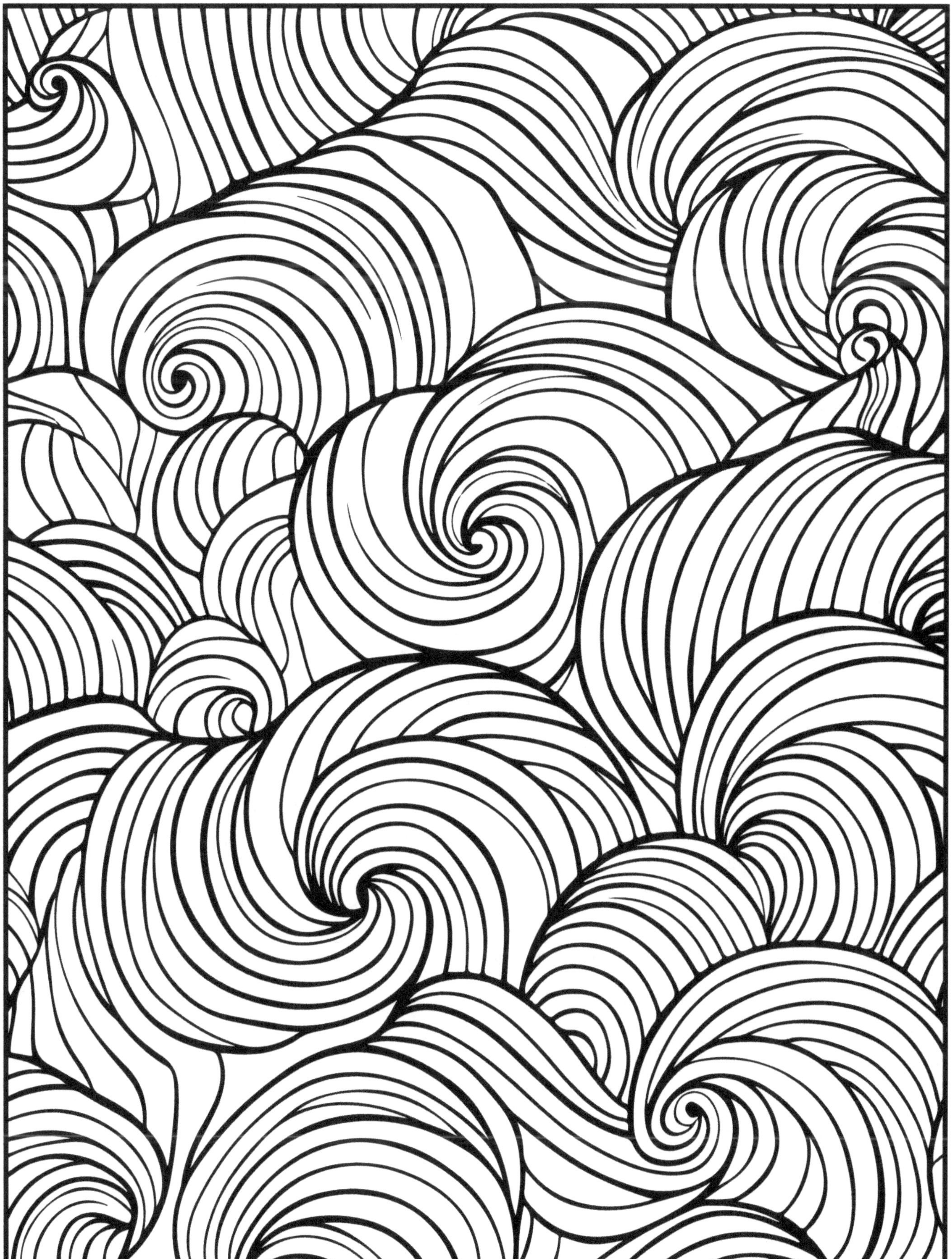

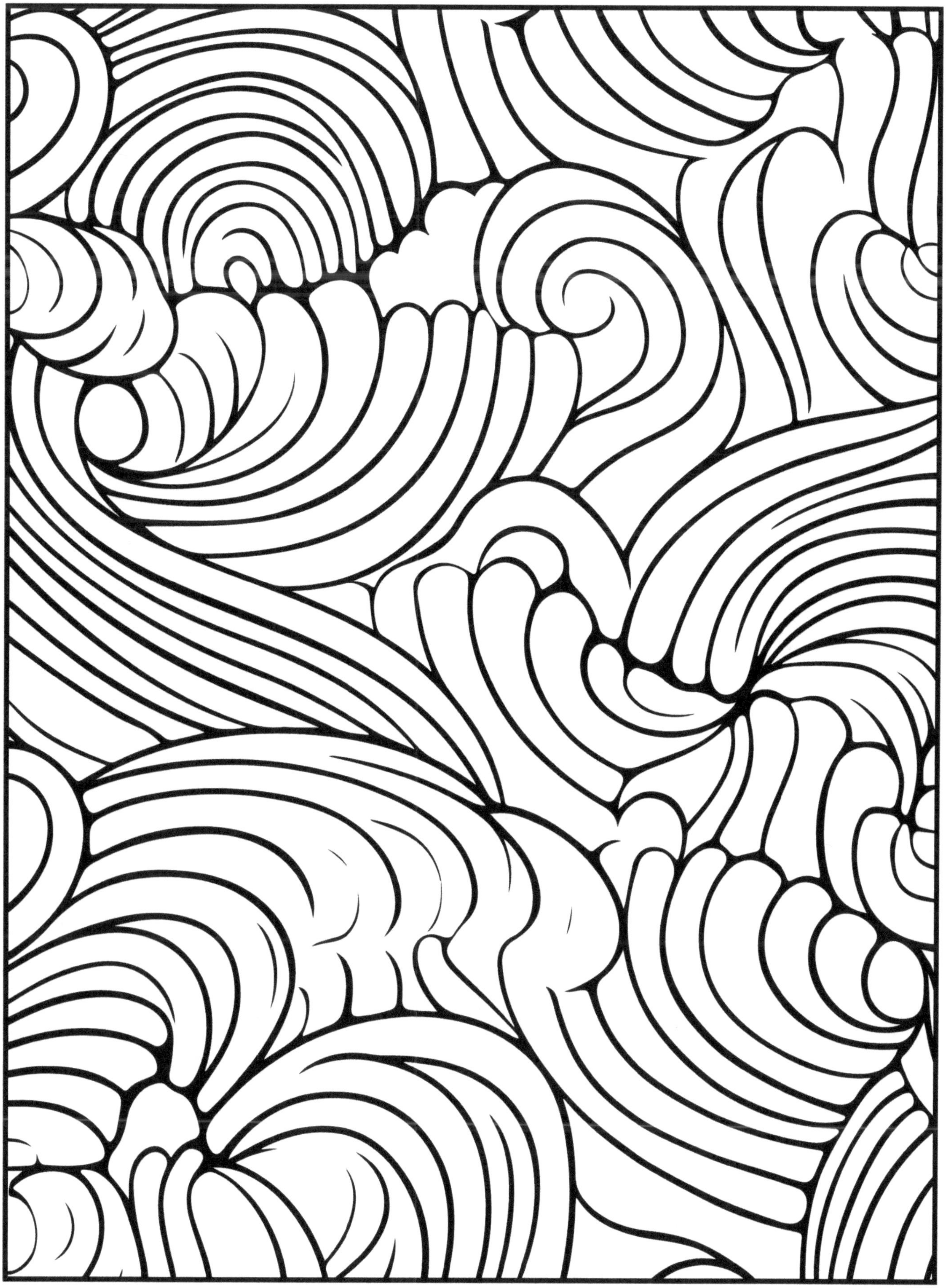

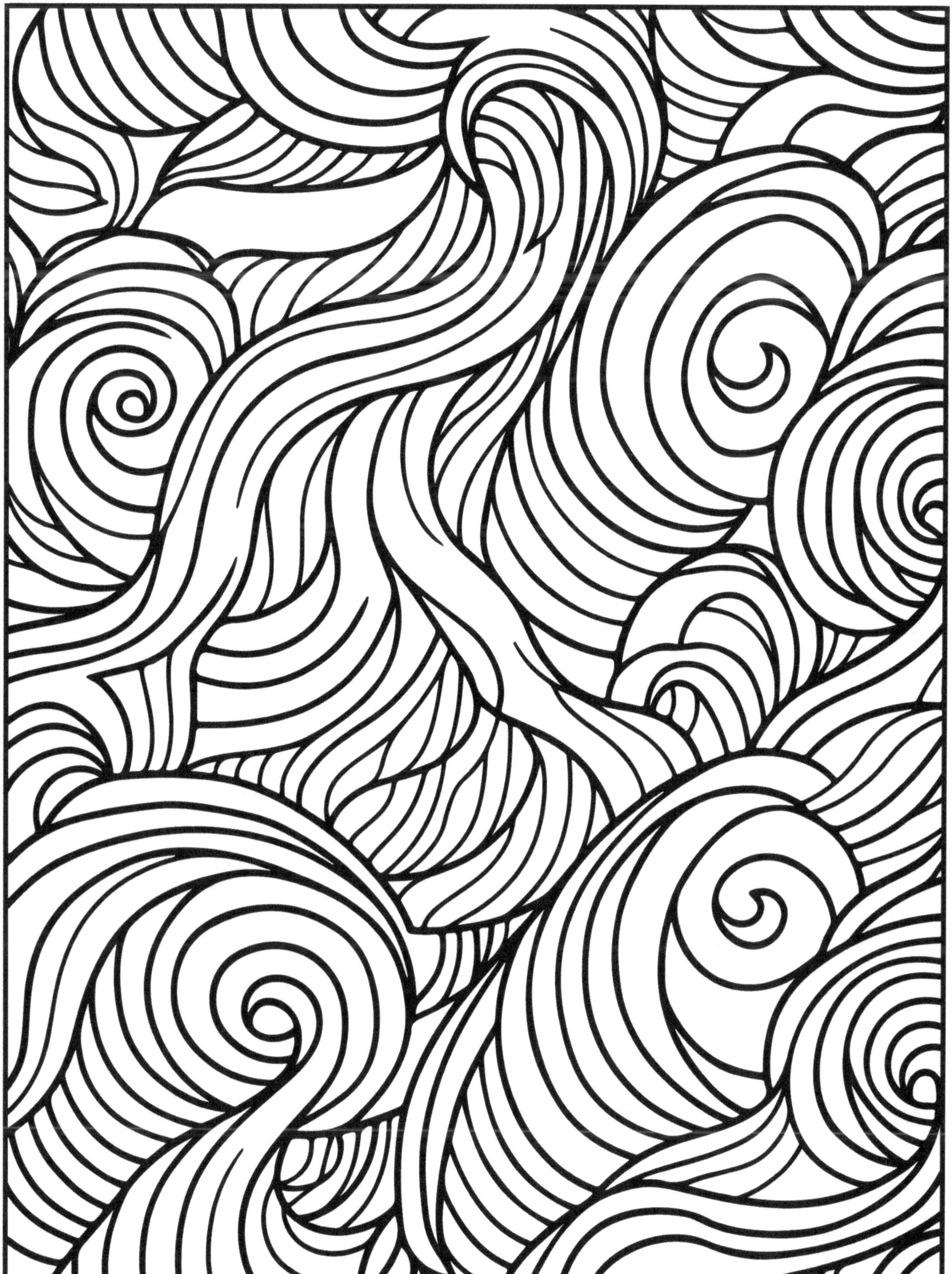

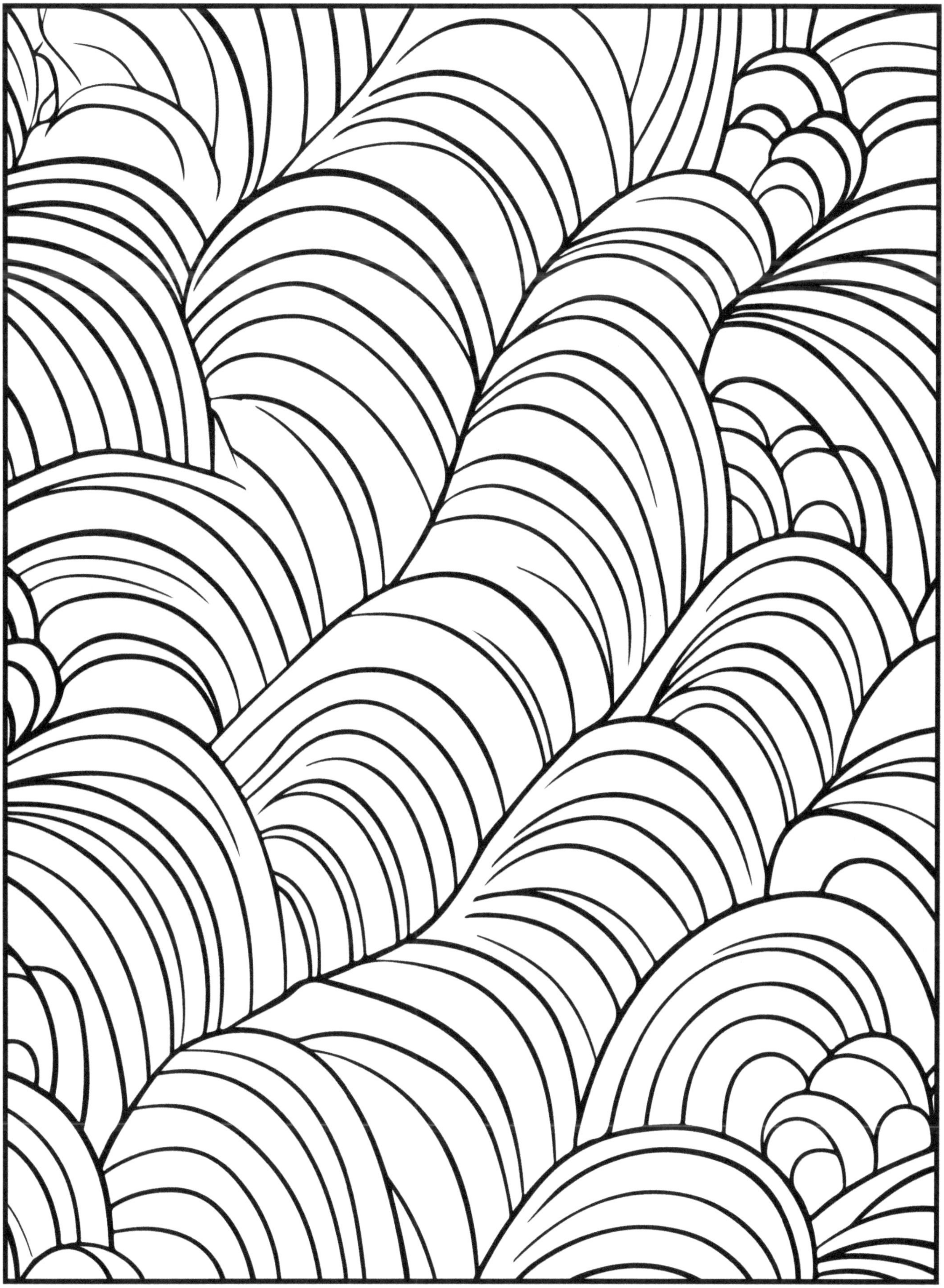

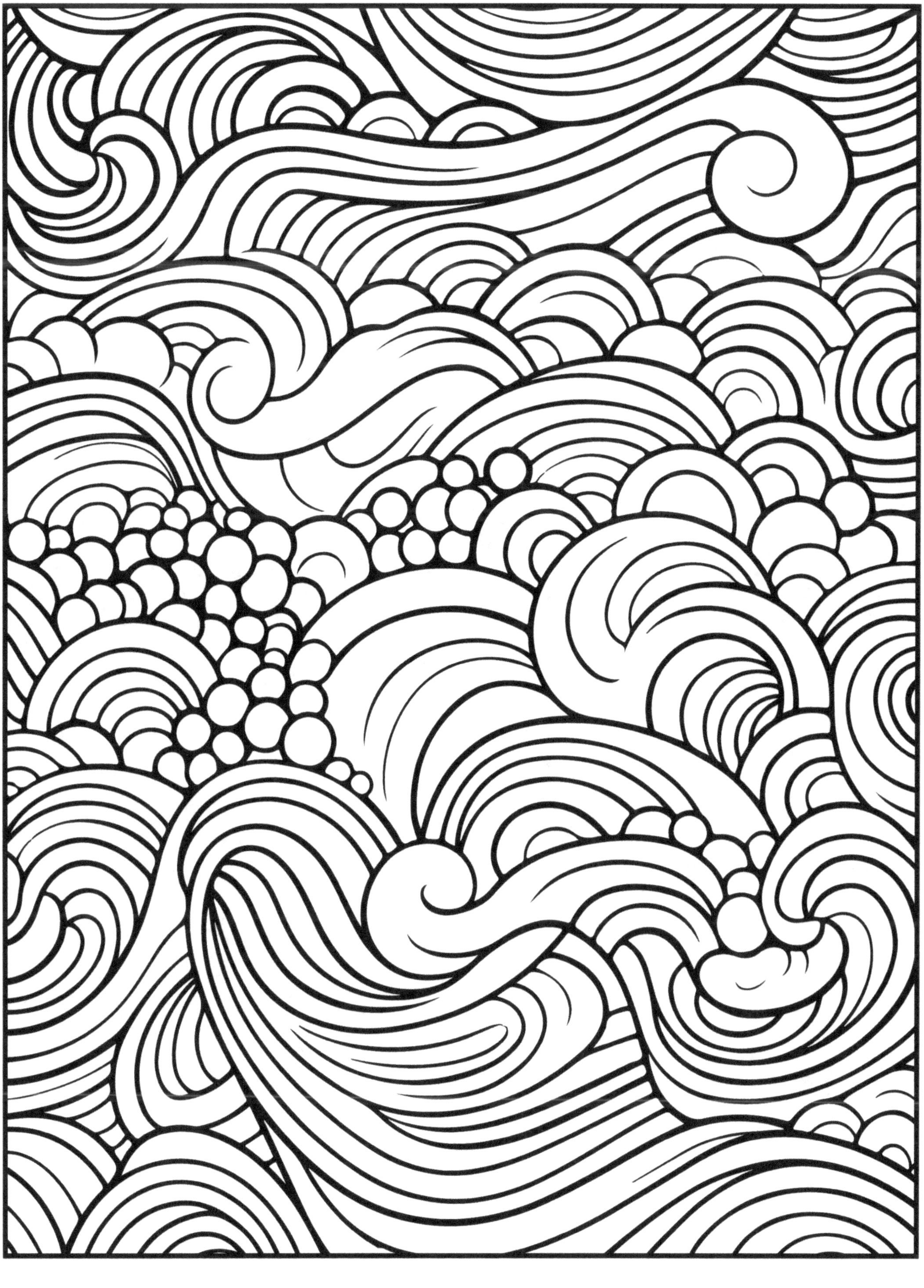

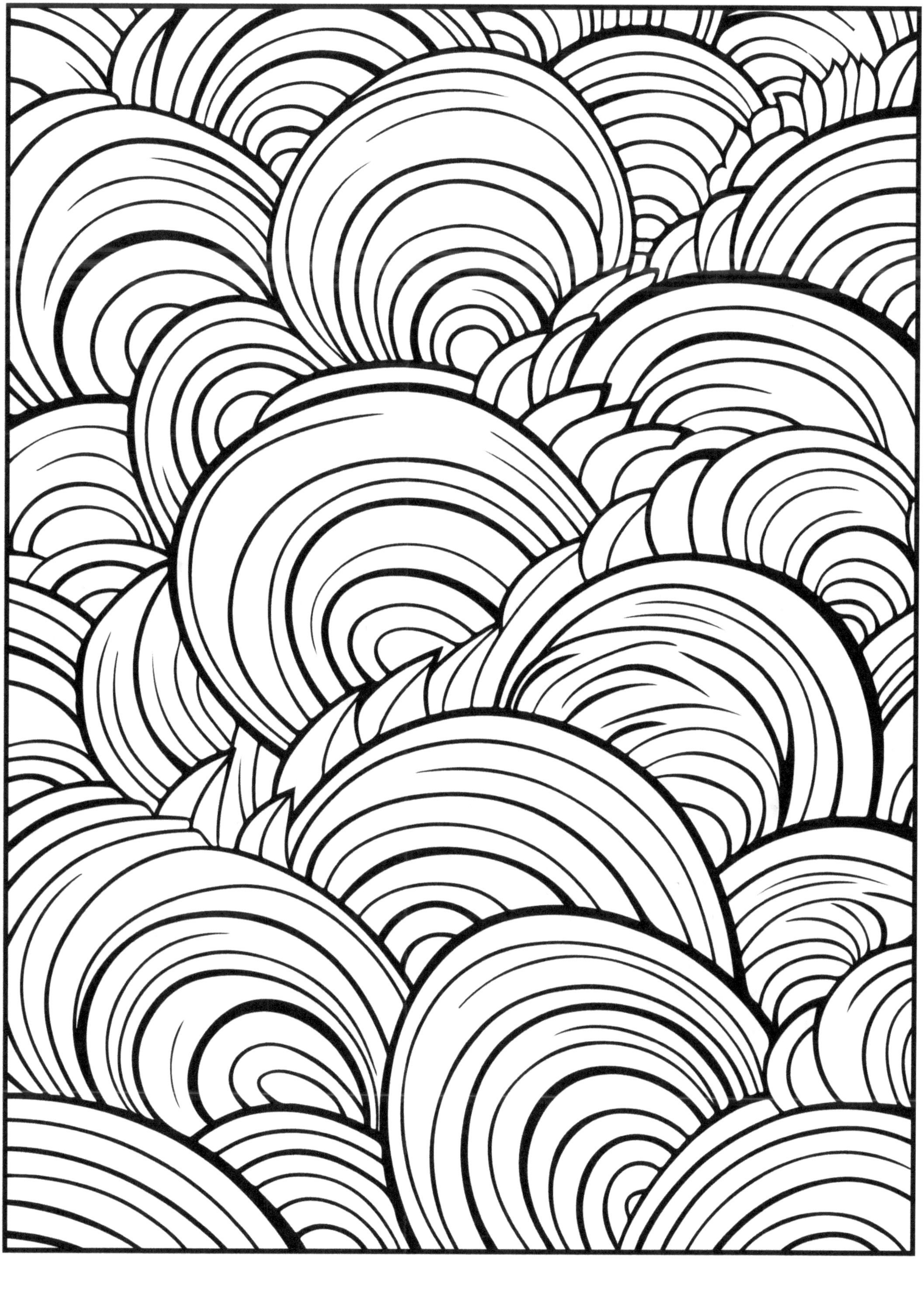

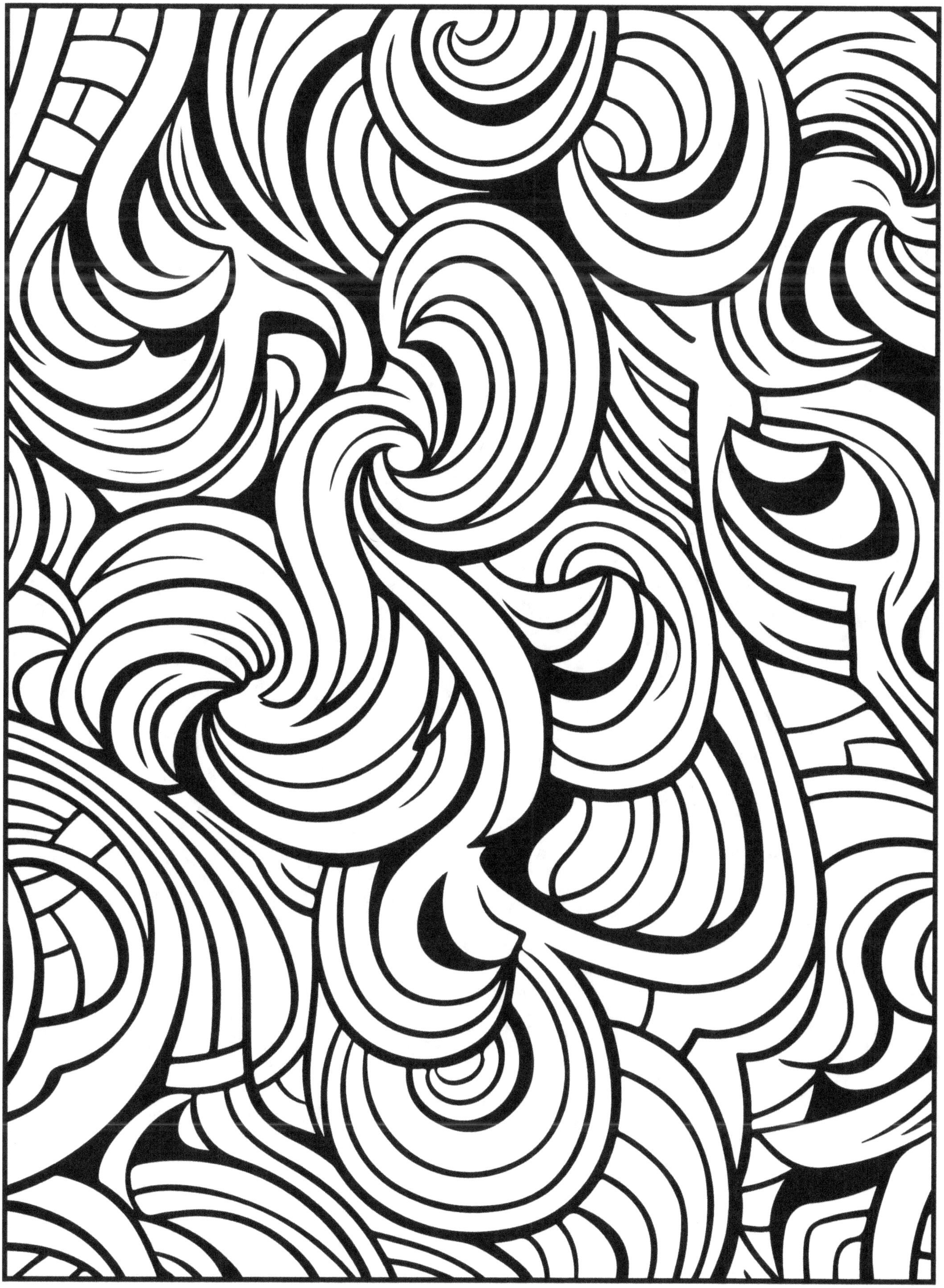

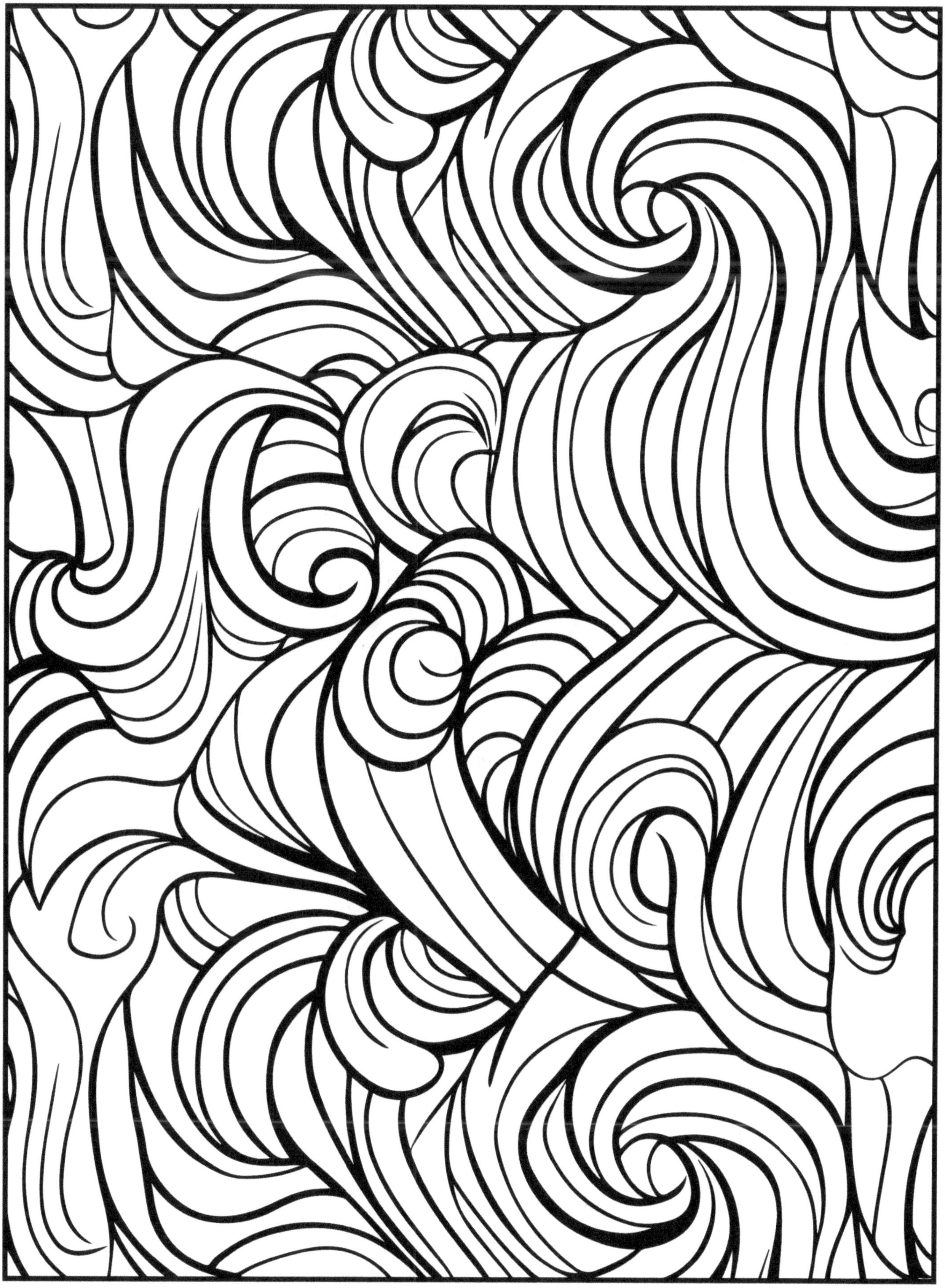

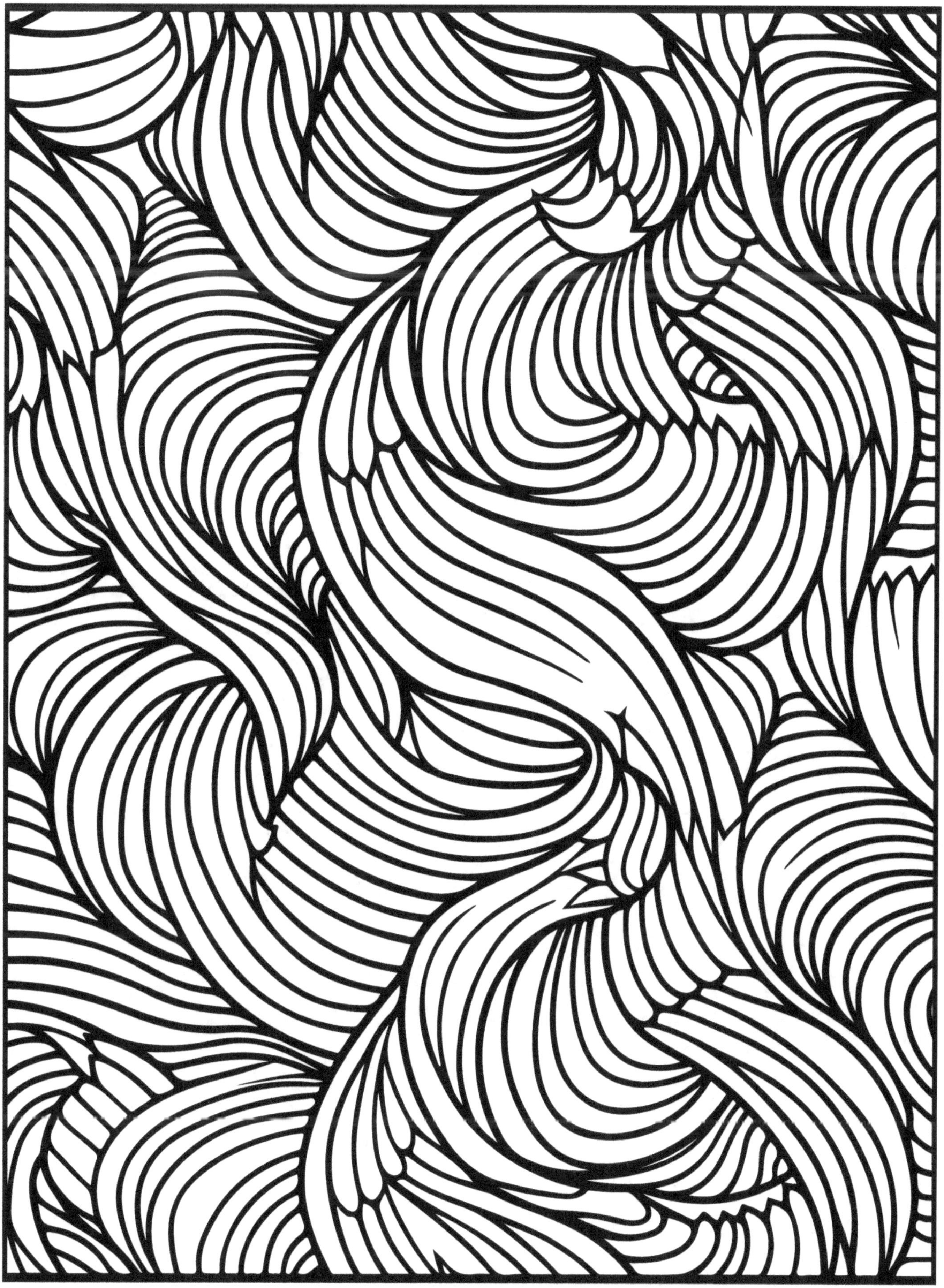

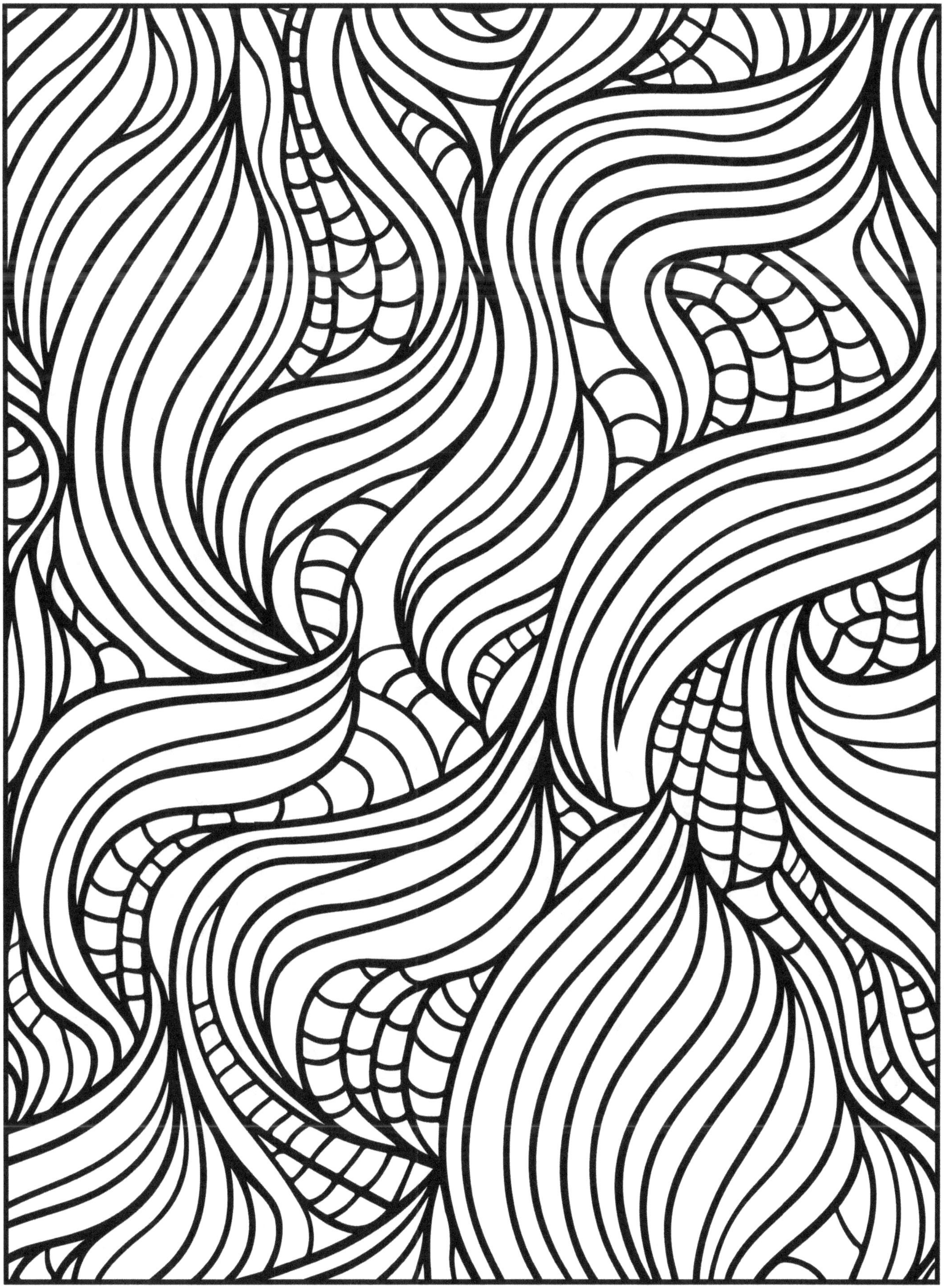

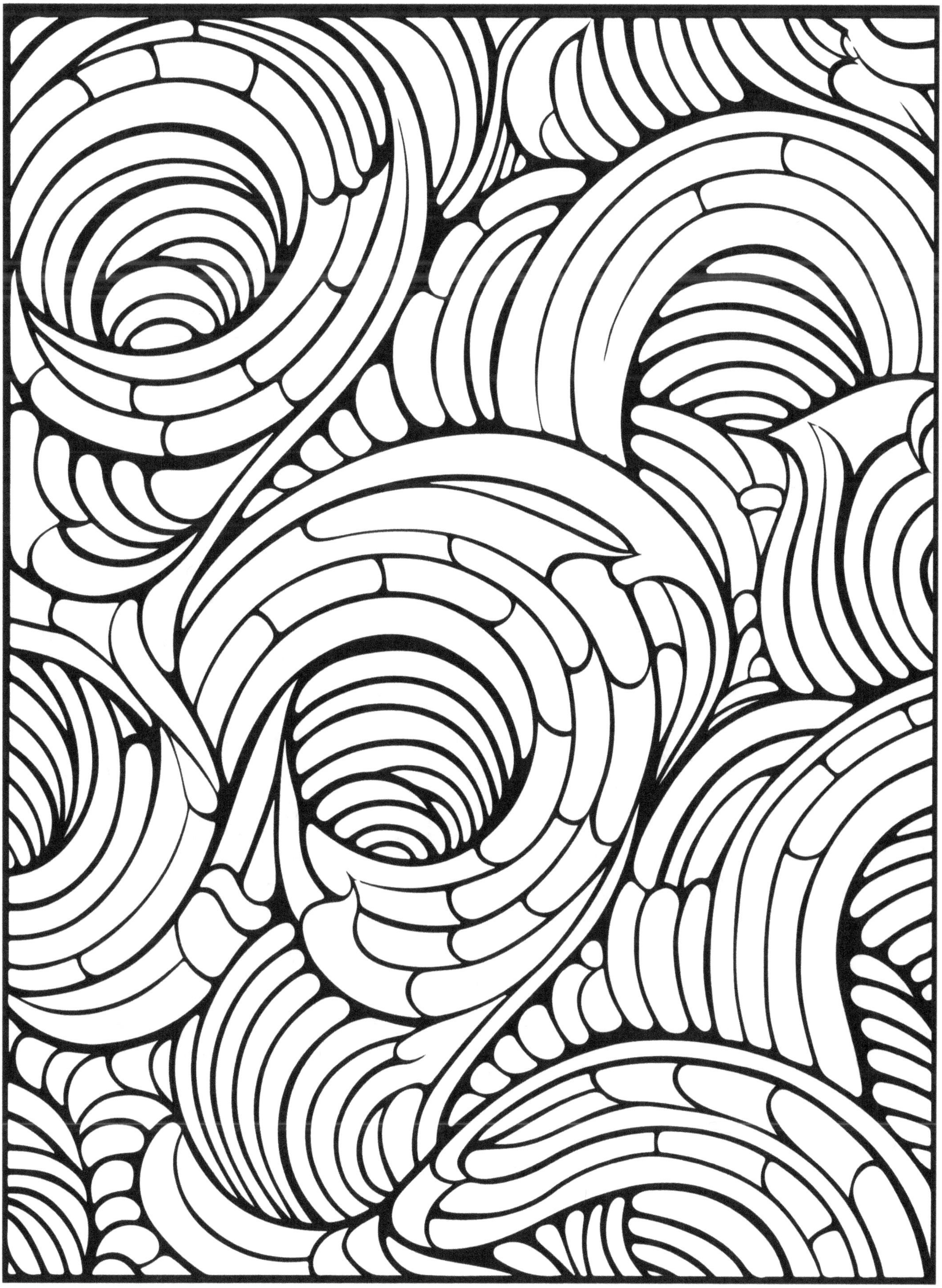

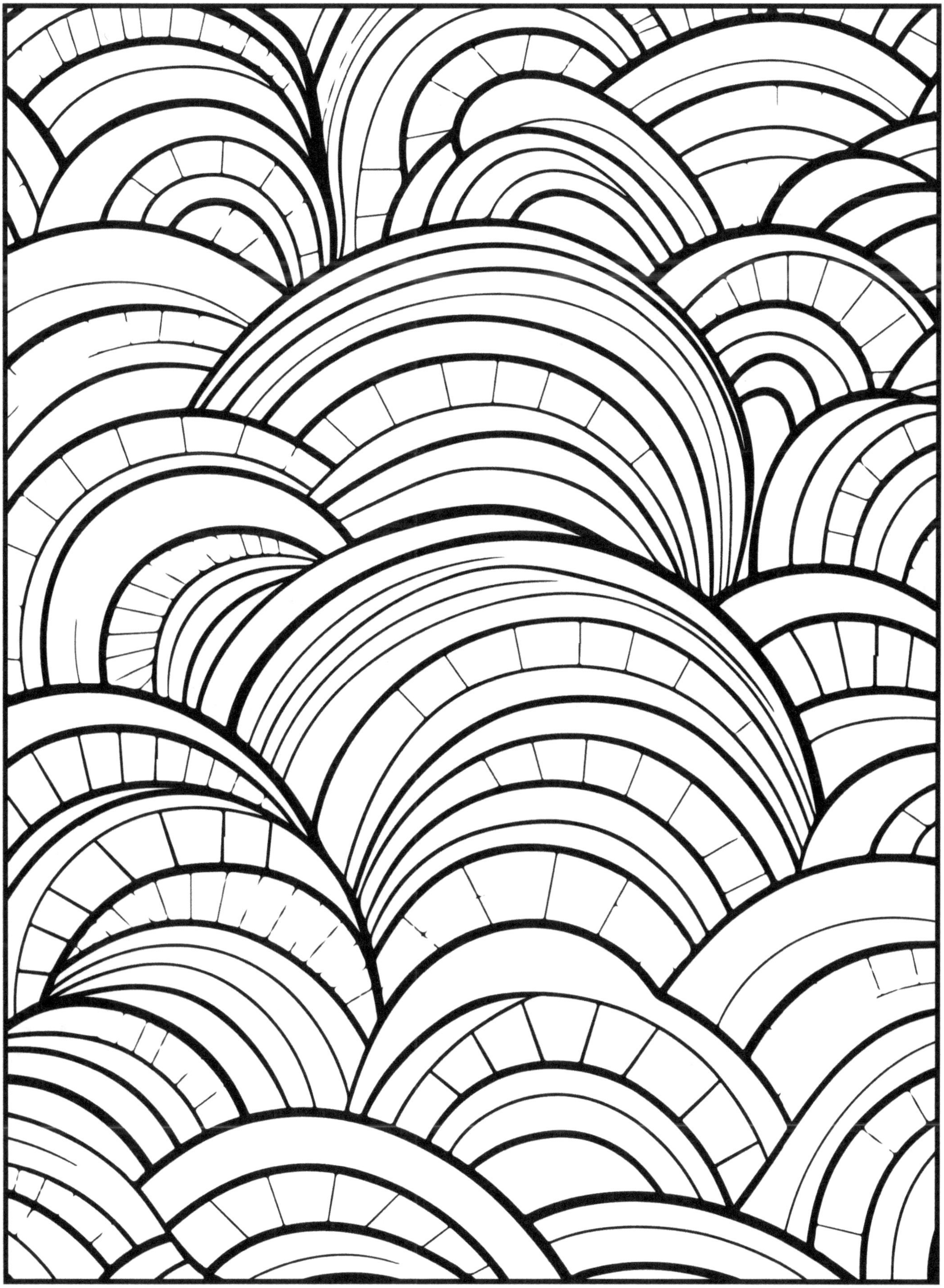

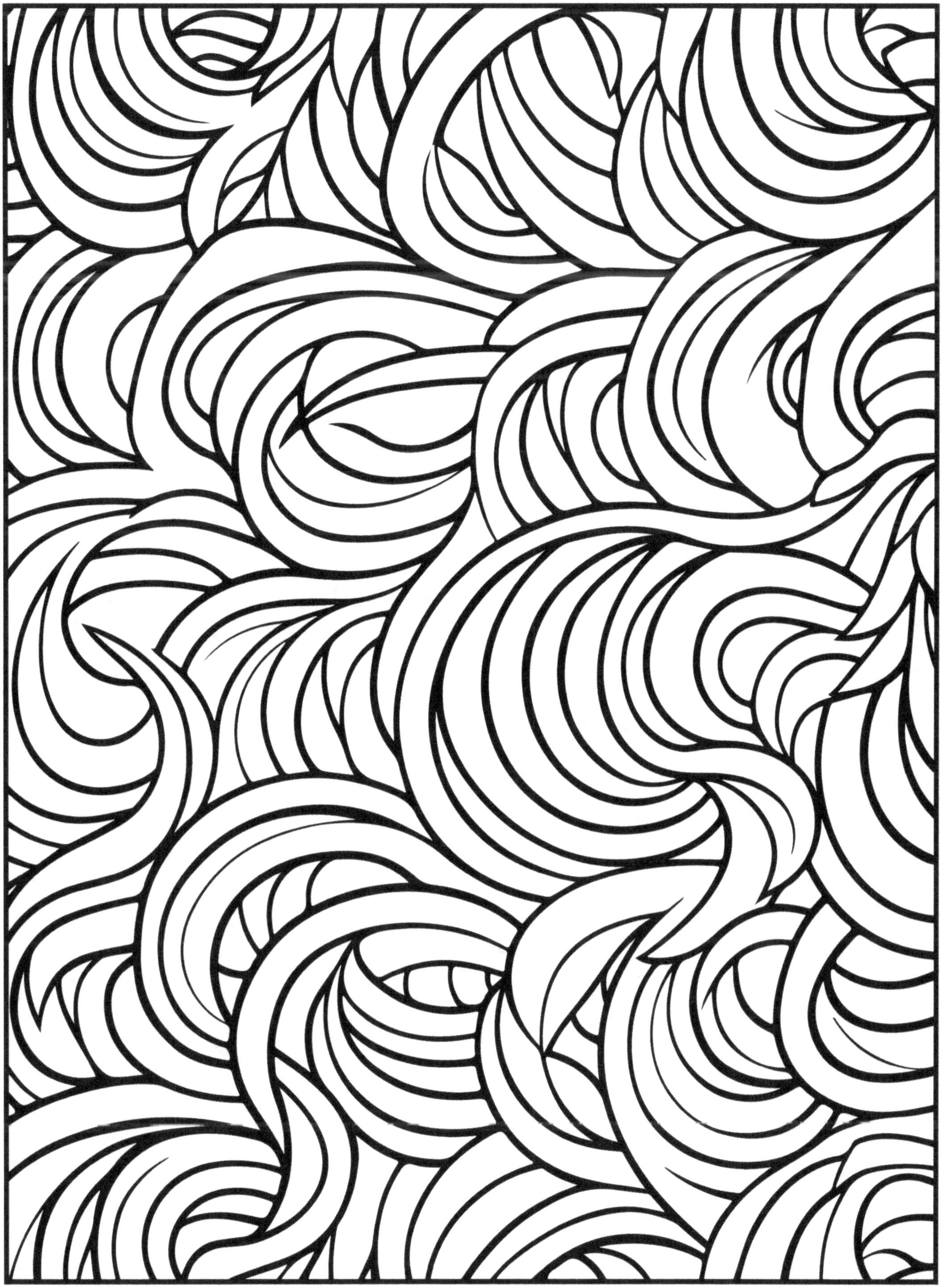

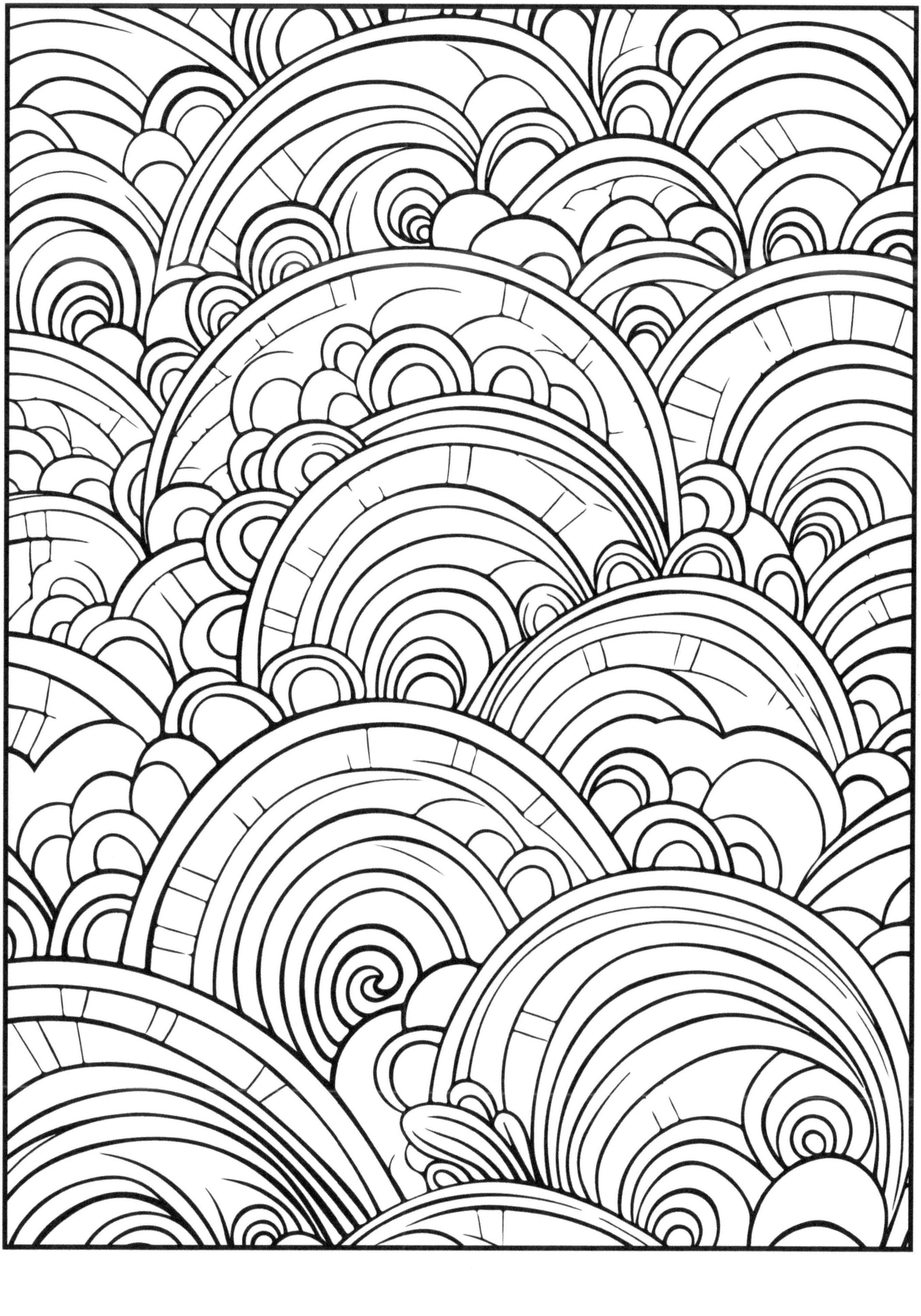

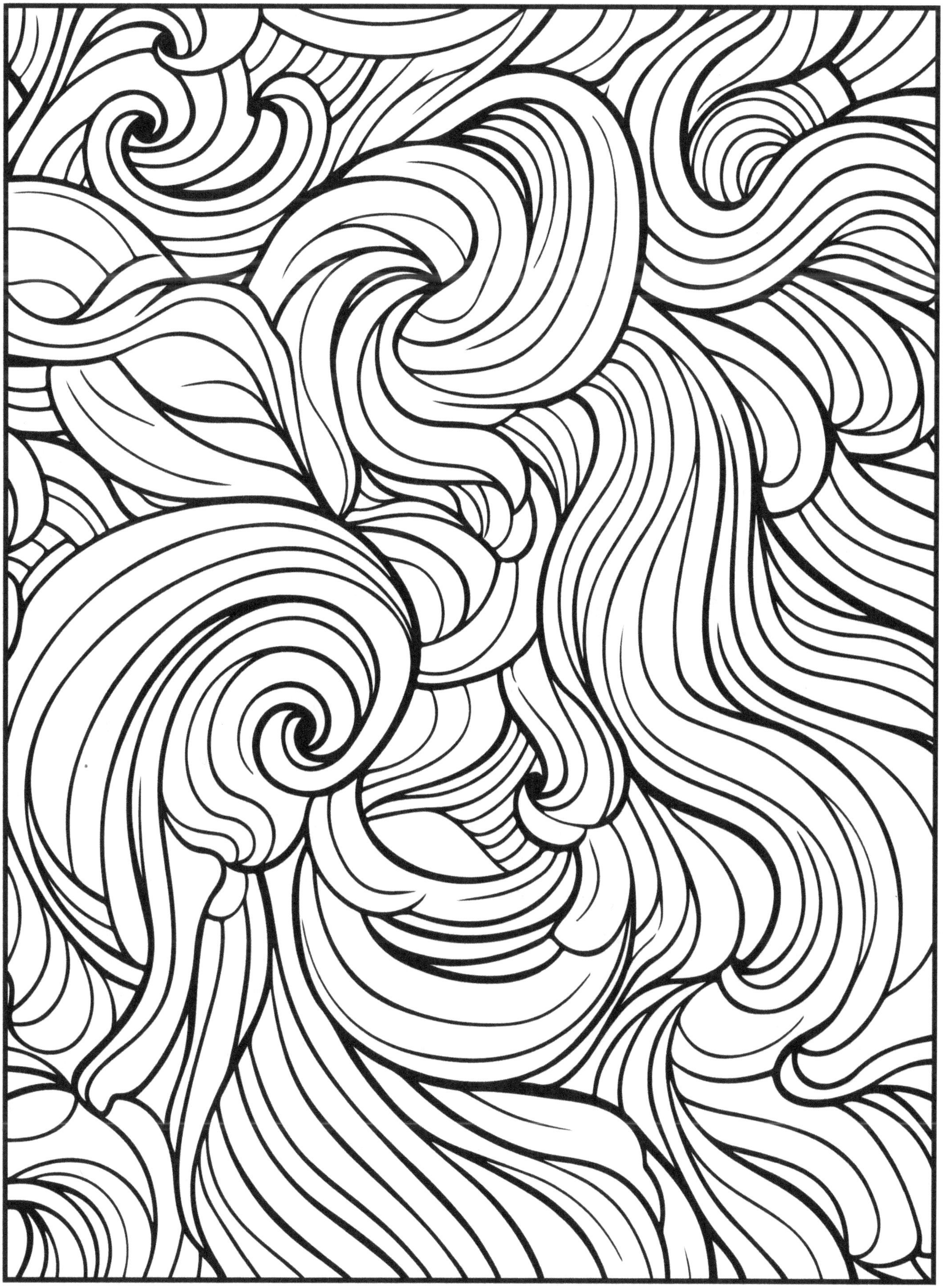

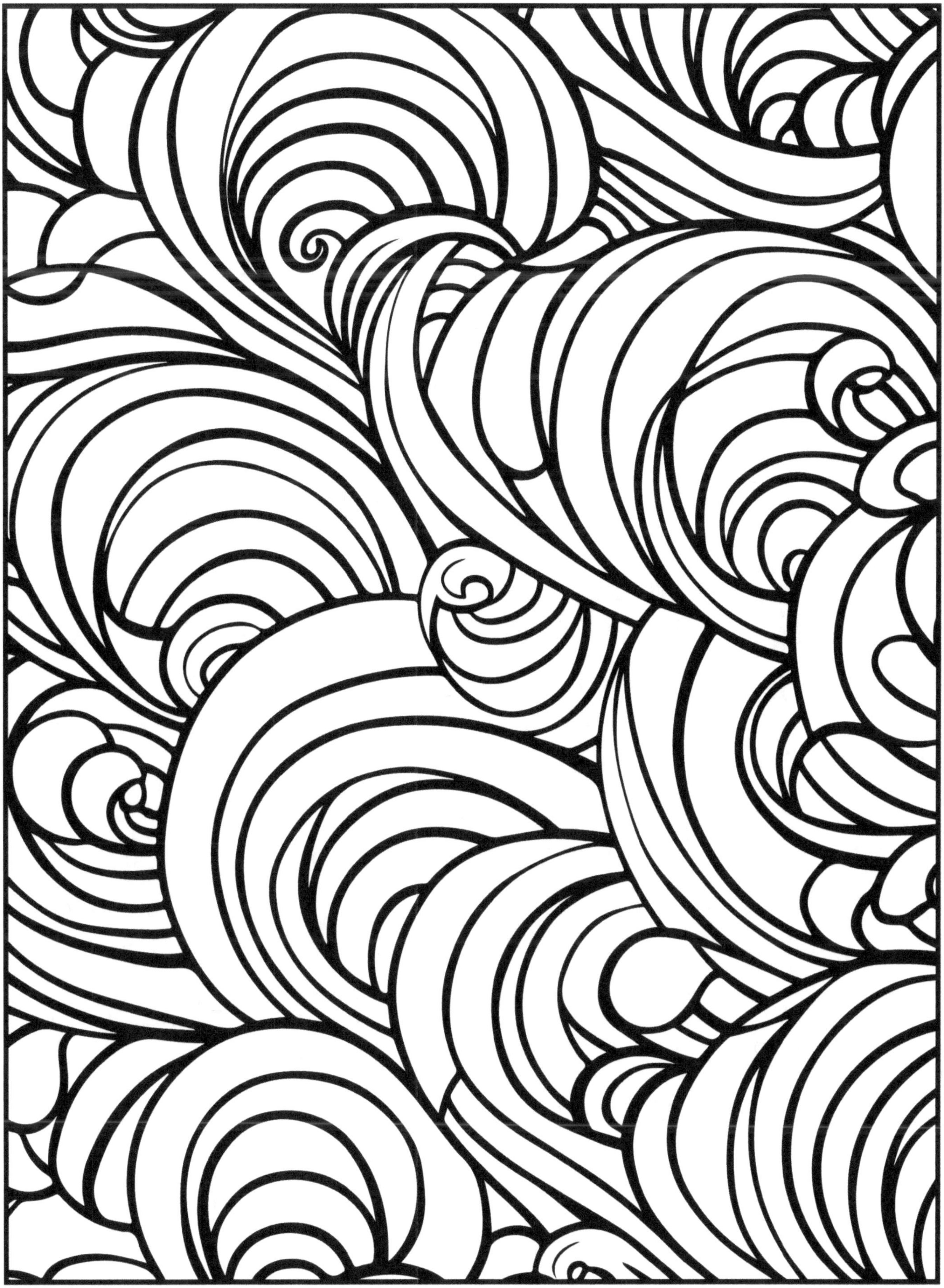

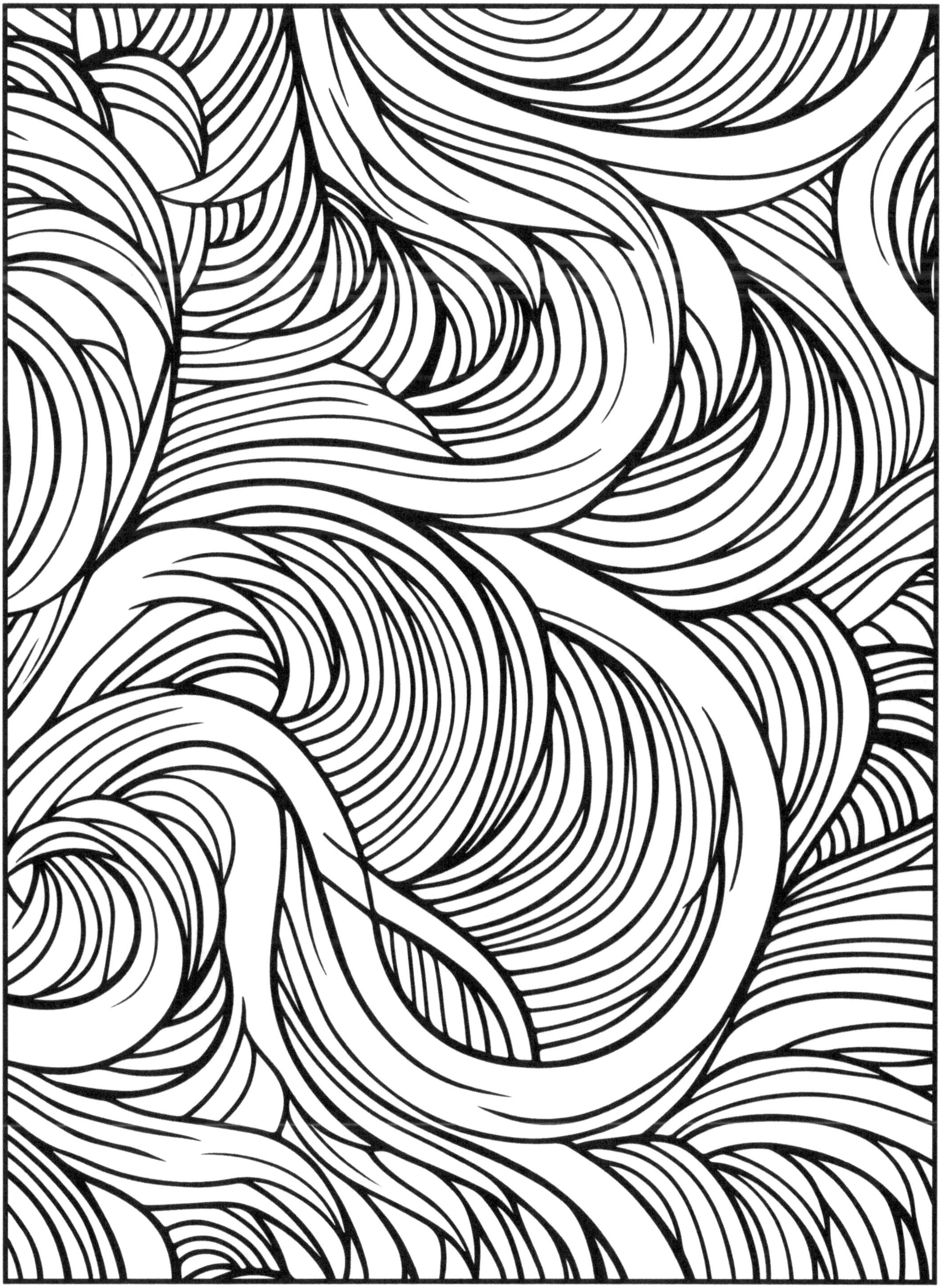

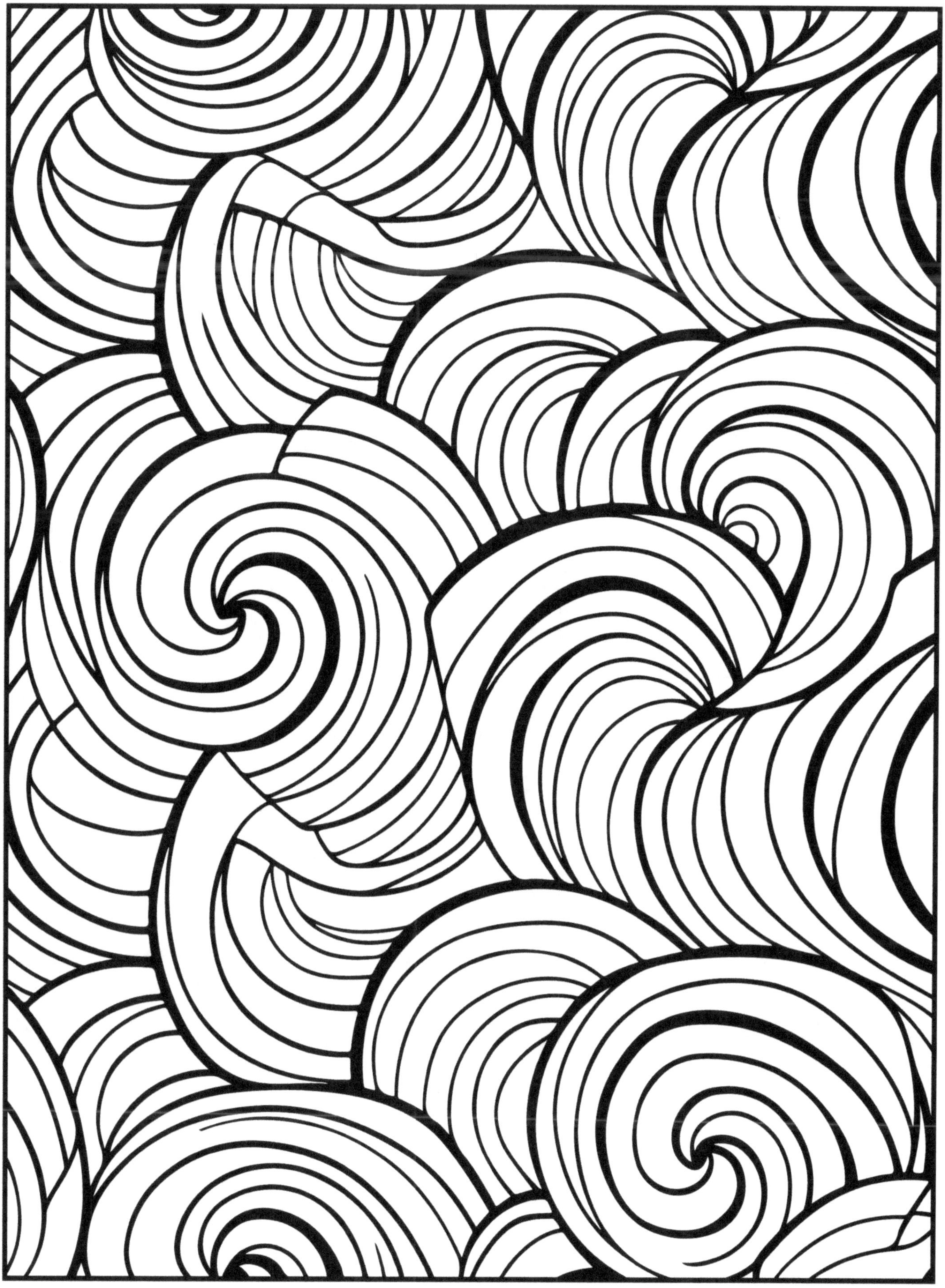

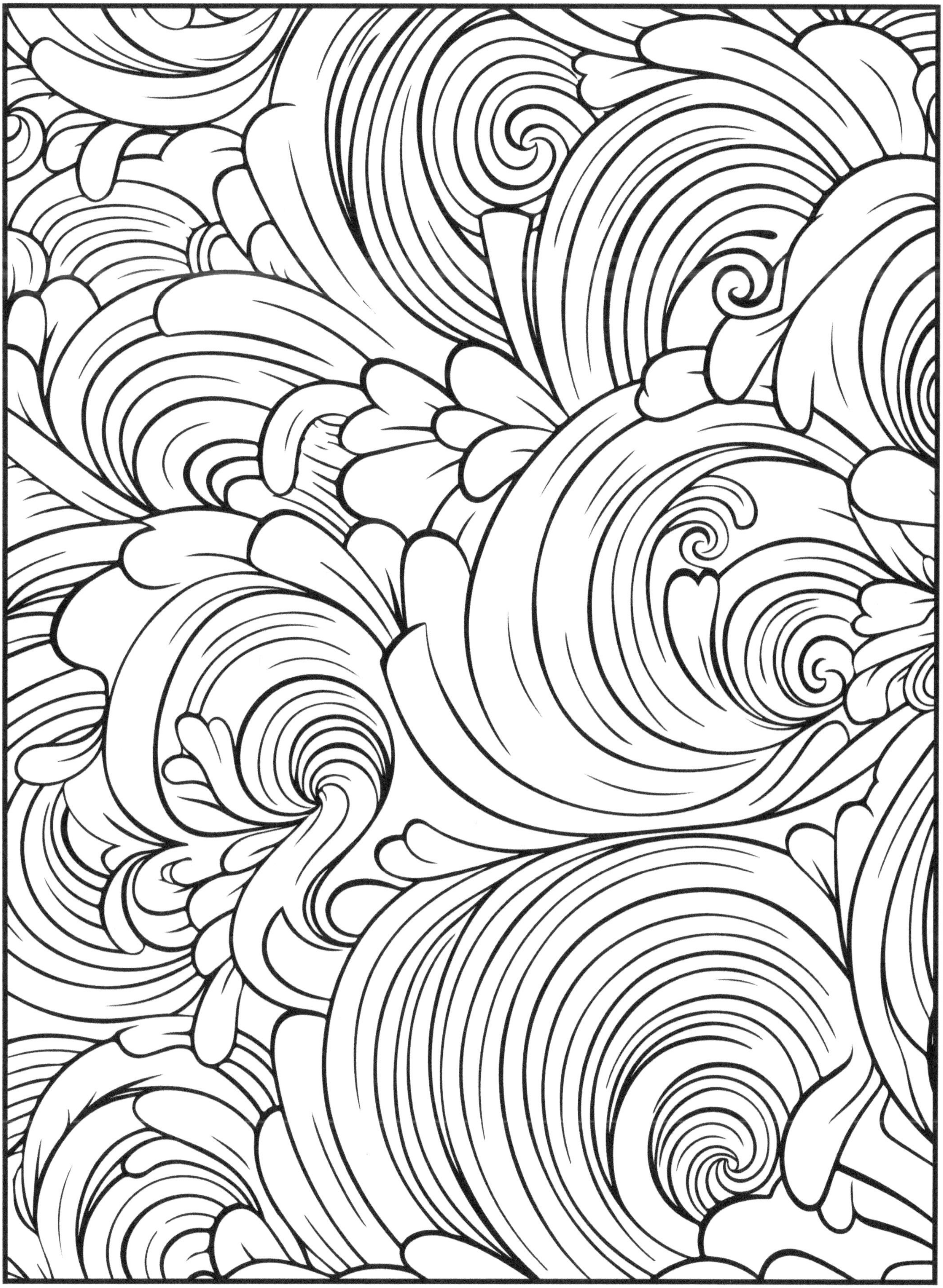

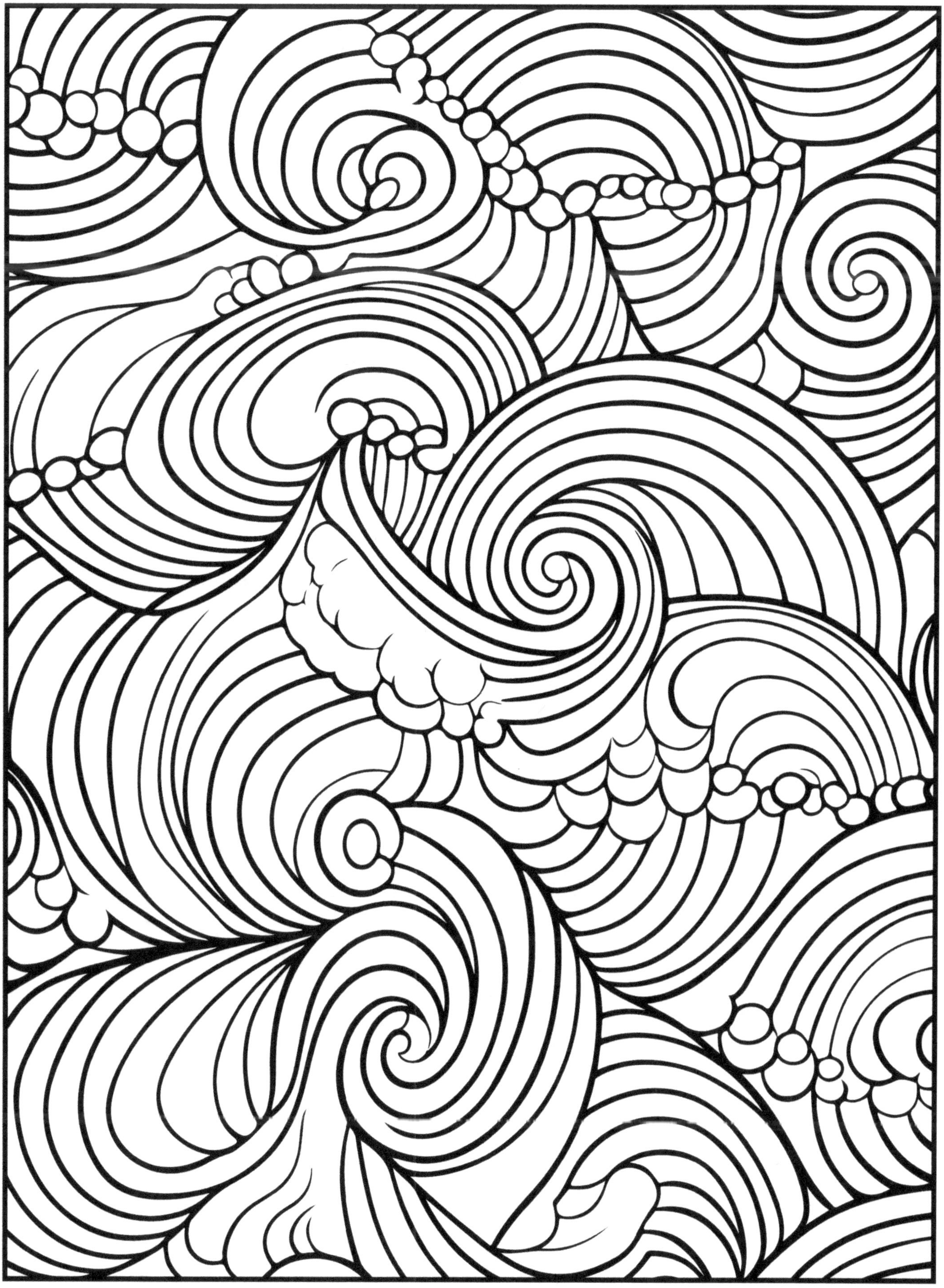

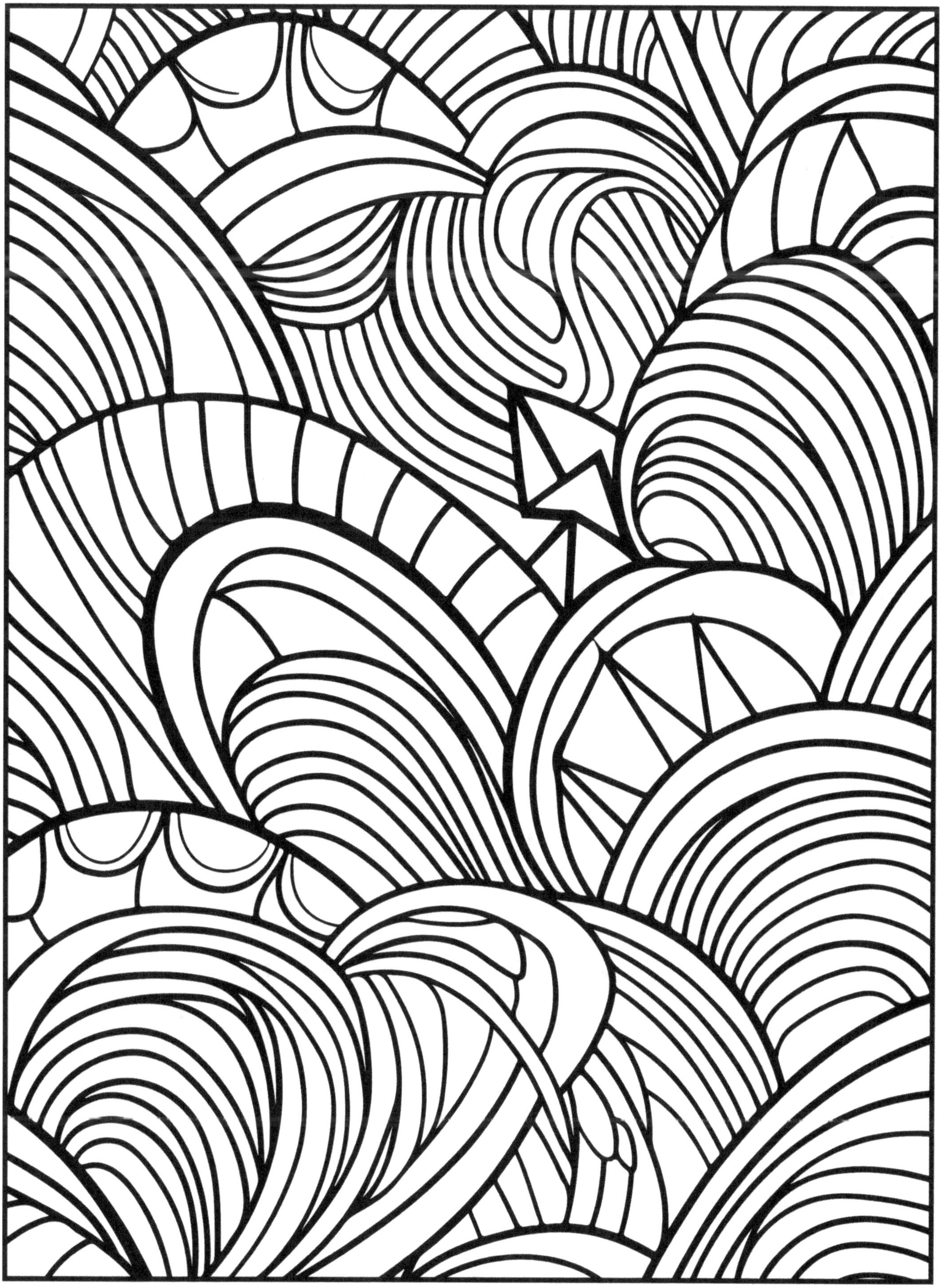

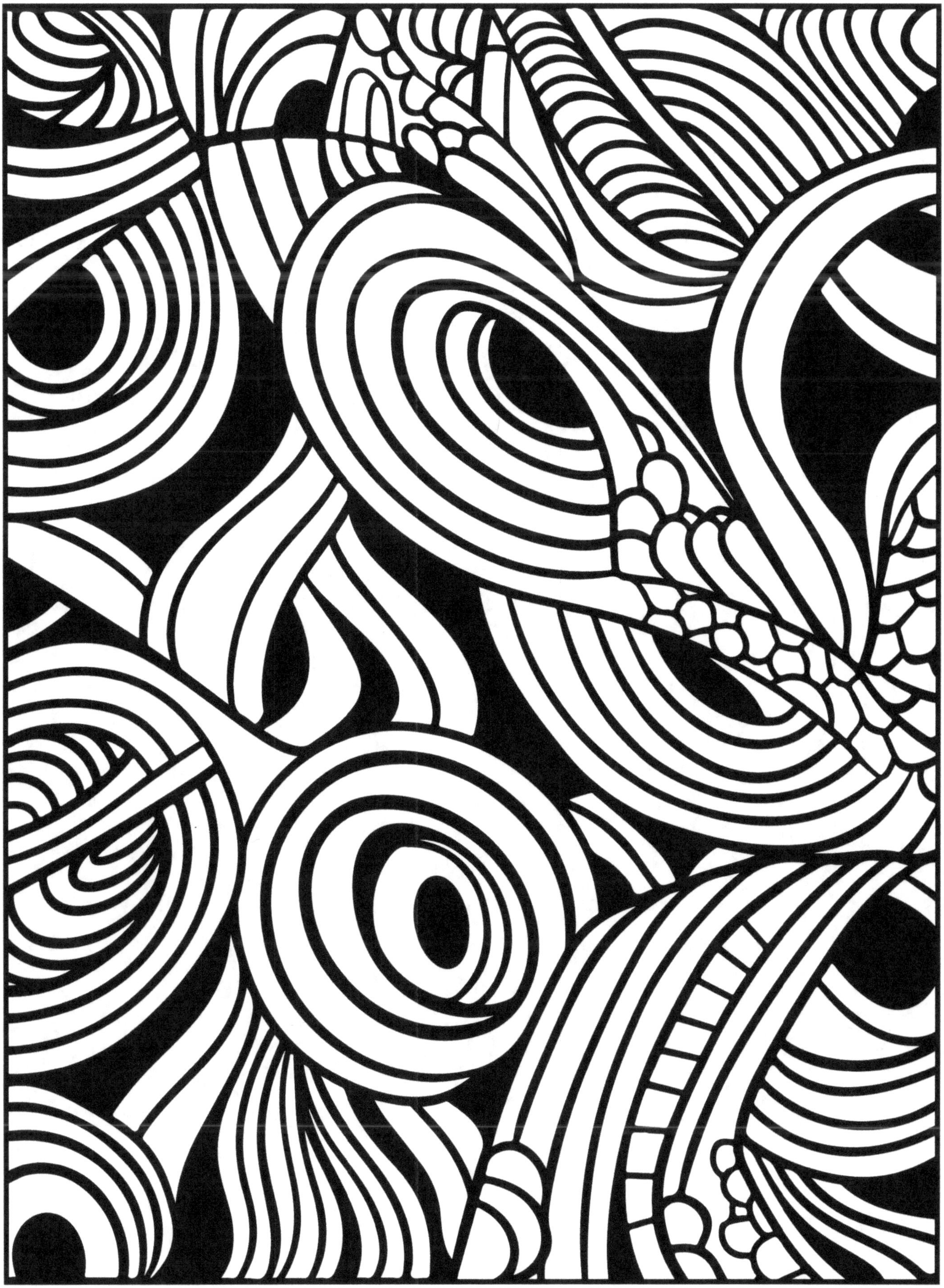

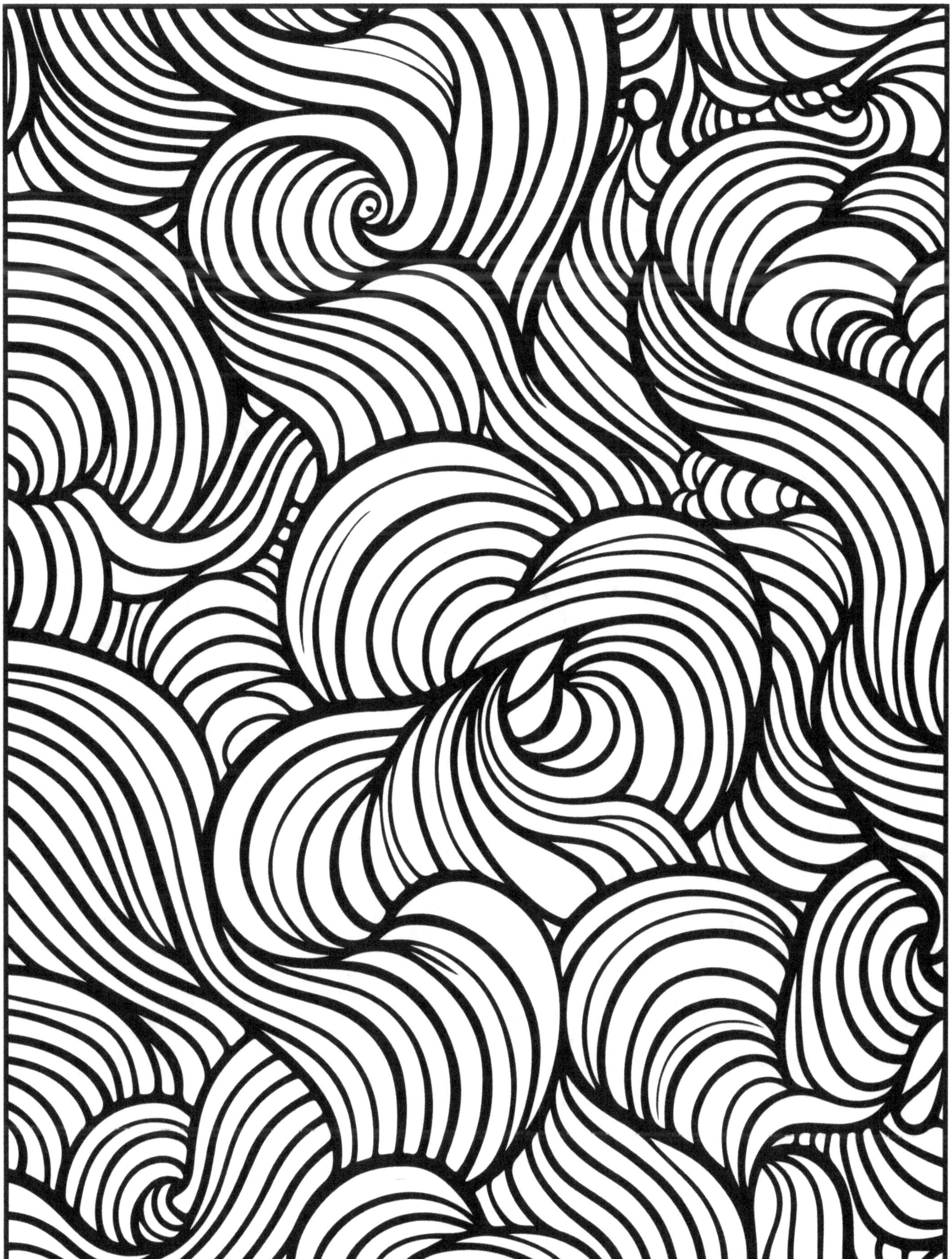

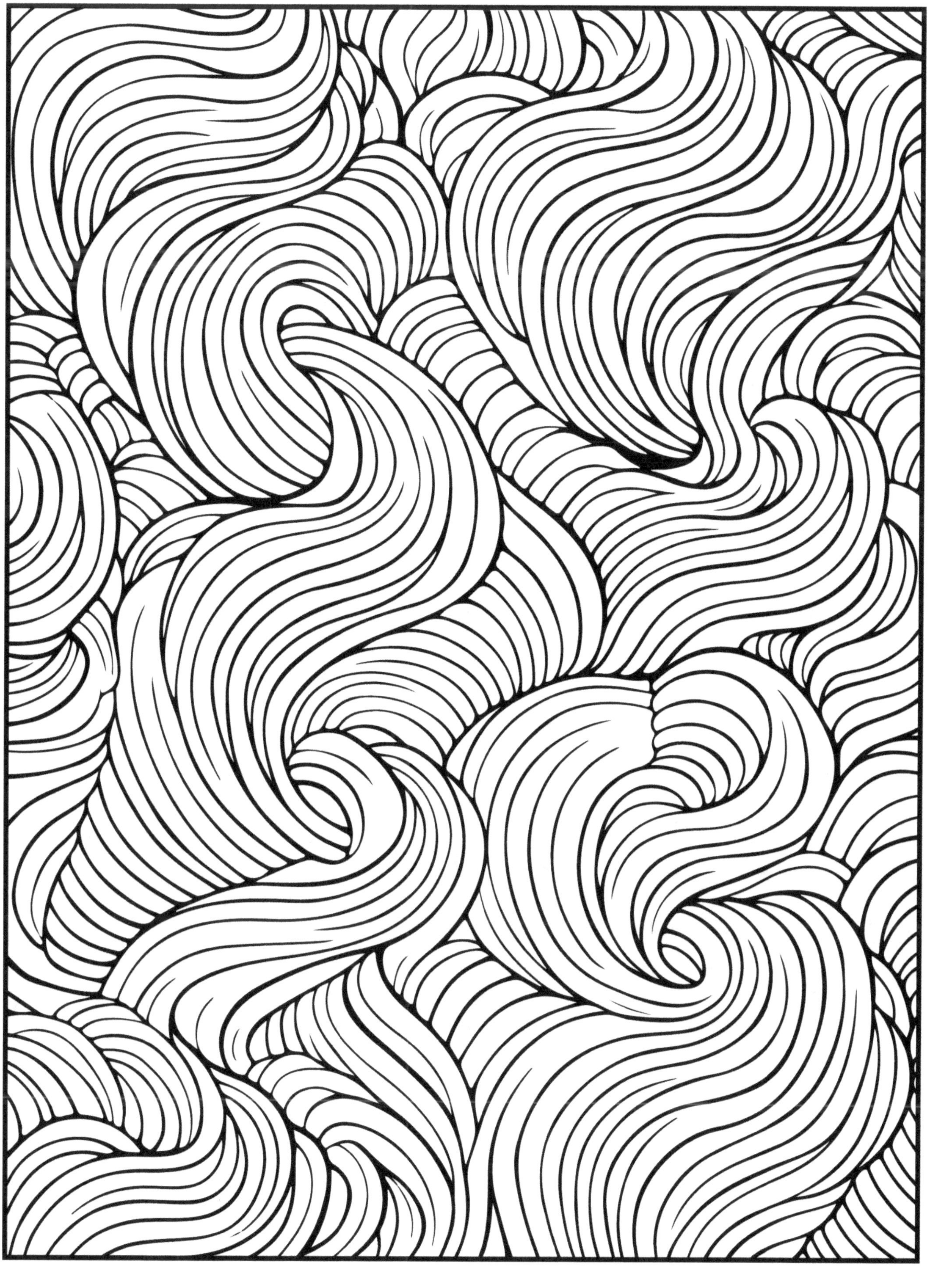

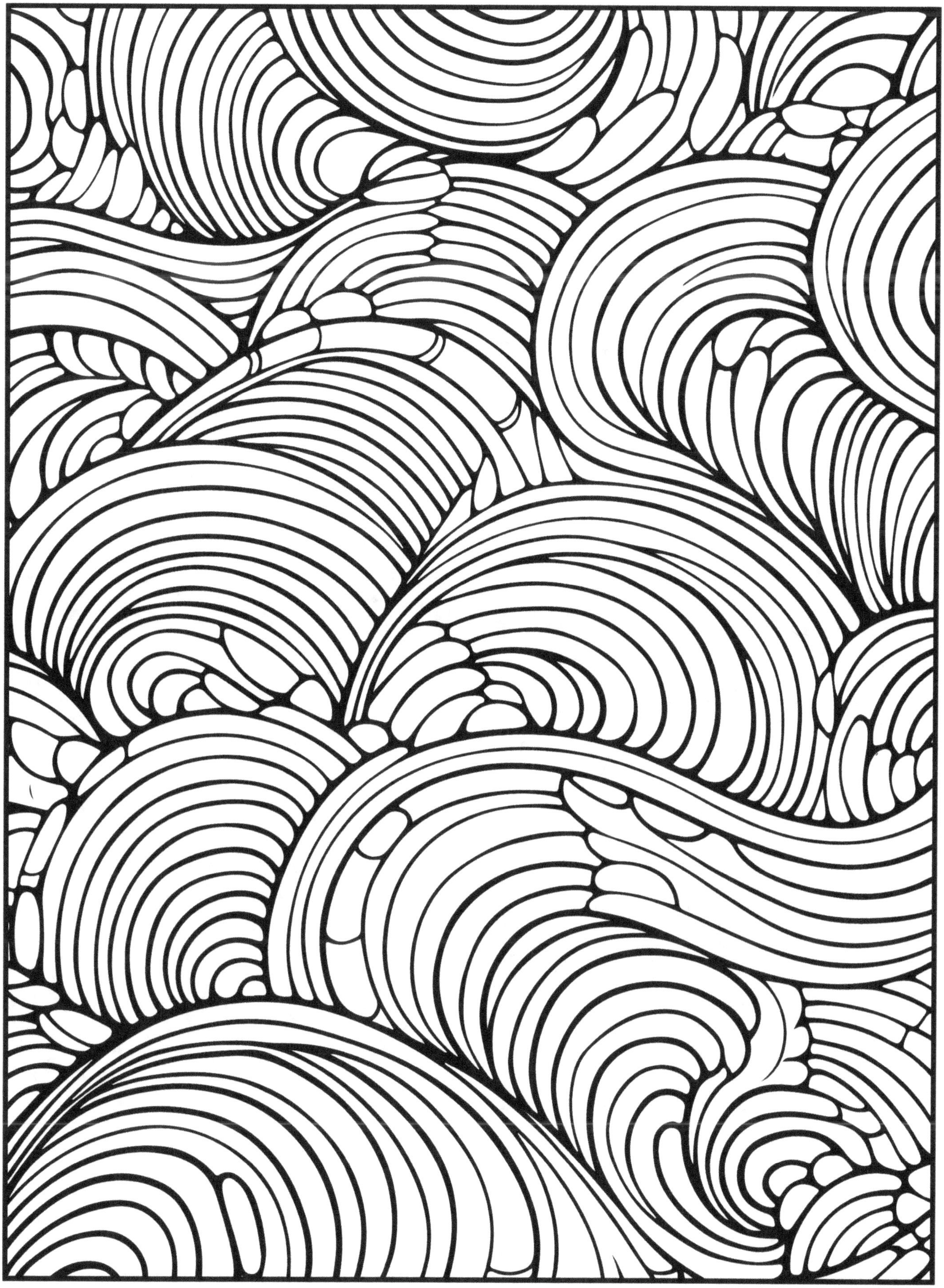

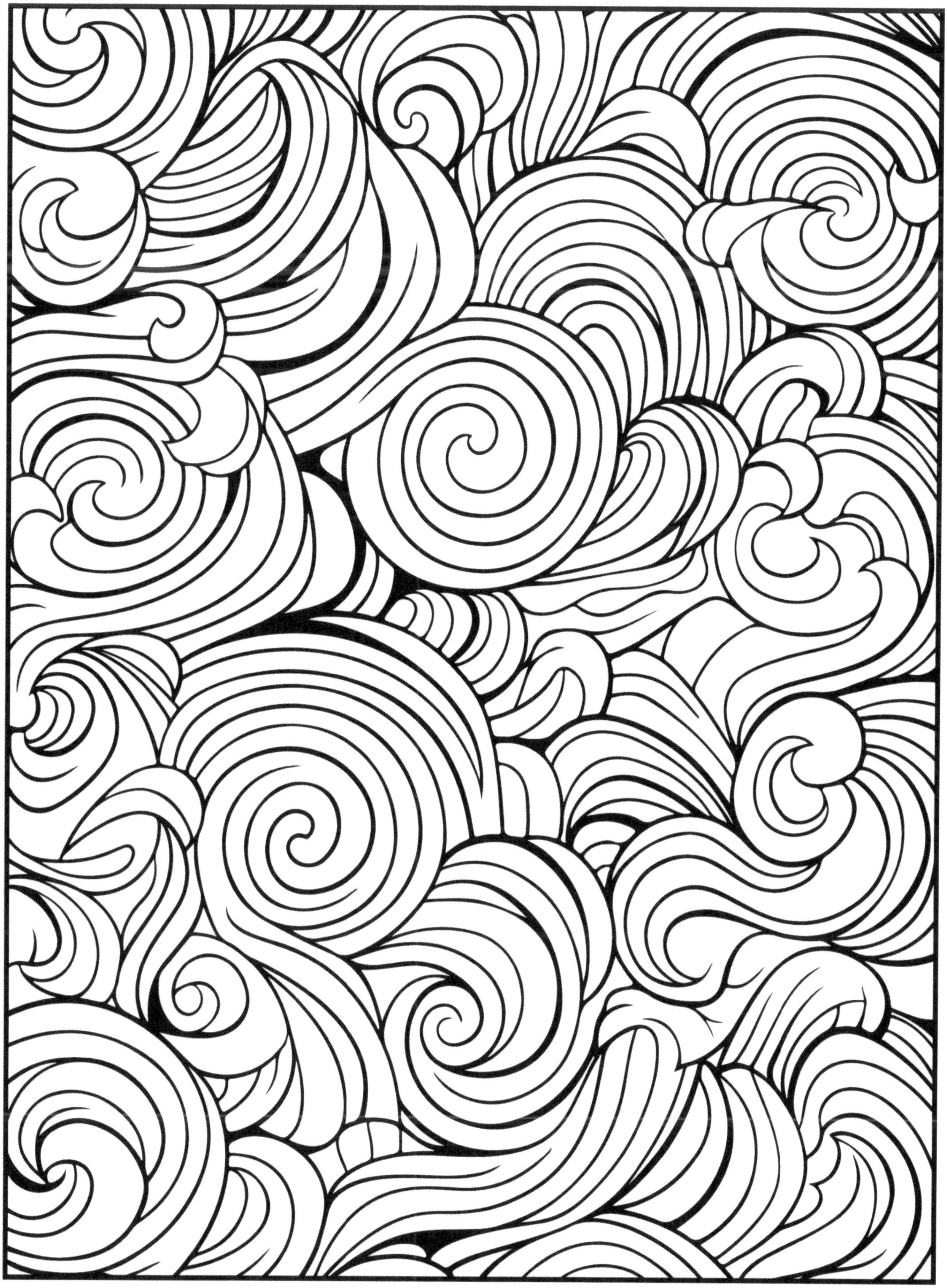

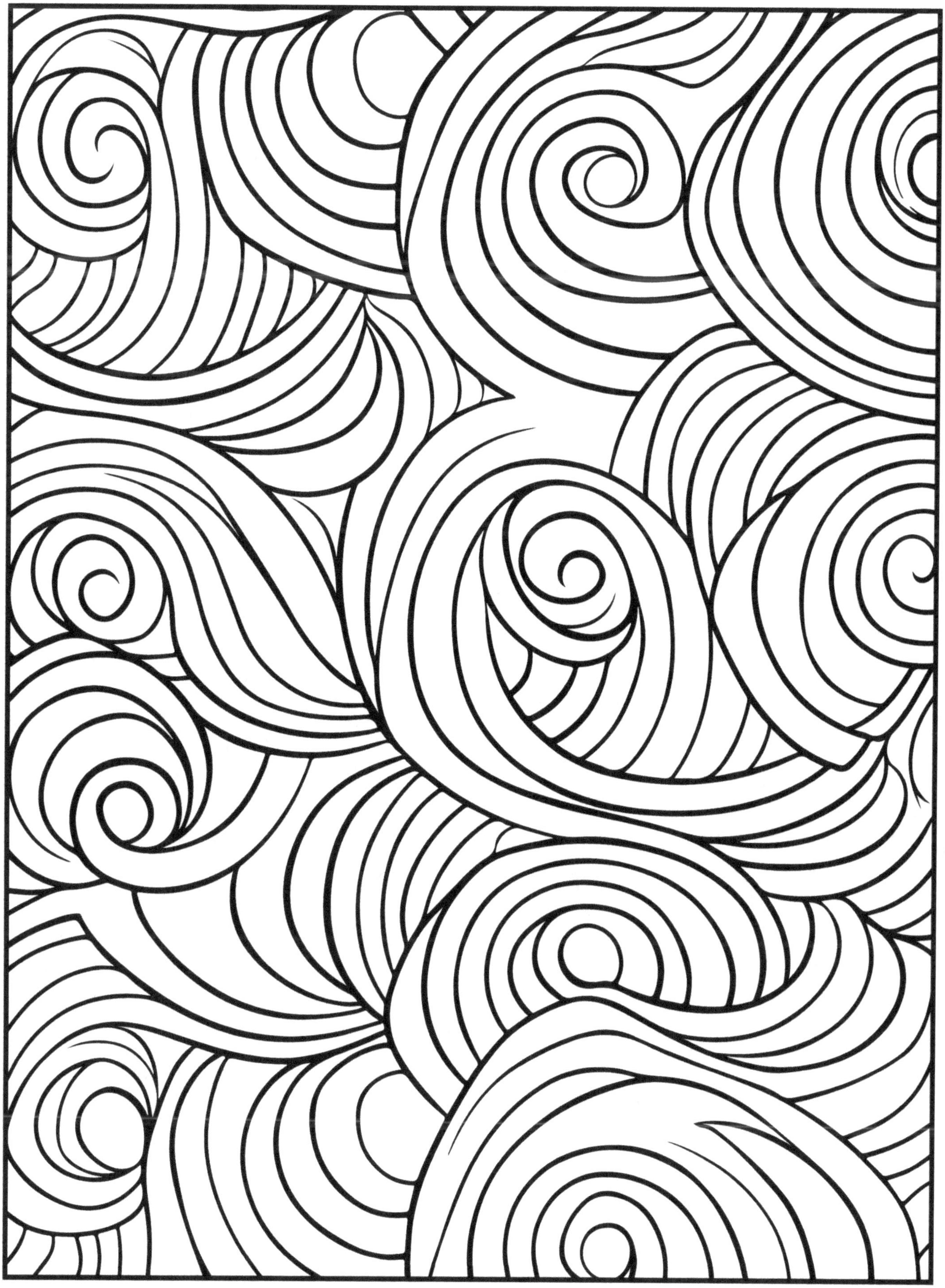

www.ingramcontent.com/pod-product-compliance
Lightning Source LLC
Chambersburg PA
CBHW082112220526
45472CB00009B/2149
9798327759077